MY GREATEST DAY

50 PEOPLE
50 GREAT MOMENTS

MY
GREATEST
DAY

50 PEOPLE
50 GREAT MOMENTS

SCOTT MORRISON

FOREWORD BY RON MACLEAN

CBC

KEY PORTER BOOKS

Library and Archives Canada Cataloguing in Publication

Morrison, Scott
      My greatest day / Scott Morrison.
At head of title: Hockey night in Canada.
ISBN 978-1-55470-086-8
      1. National Hockey League—Biography. 2. National Hockey
League—Miscellanea. I. Title.
GV847.8.N3M673 2008   796.962092   C2008-902275-0

The publisher gratefully acknowledges the support of the Canada
Council for the Arts and the Ontario Arts Council for its publishing
program. We acknowledge the support of the Government of
Ontario through the Ontario Media Development Corporation's
Ontario Book Initiative.

We acknowledge the financial support of the Government of
Canada through the Book Publishing Industry Development
Program (BPIDP) for our publishing activities.

Key Porter Books Limited
Six Adelaide Street East, Tenth Floor
Toronto, Ontario
Canada M5C 1H6

www.keyporter.com

www.cbcsports.ca

Text design and electronic formatting: First Image

Printed and bound in Canada

08 09 10 11 12 5 4 3 2 1

To all my family and friends for their support, but especially to my wife Kathy—every day is a greatest day—and my son Mark, who has truly been a gift.

Acknowledgements

It's an old cliché, but it's also true. A hockey team doesn't win with one person. You win as a team. And so it is with a book project such as this. Consider the volume of the project, factor in time and timing constraints and the overall workload, and it takes more than just the name that appears on the cover to get the job done.

There are many people who deserve thanks and acknowledgement for their efforts, beginning with the 50 people whose stories appear on these pages. It wasn't easy for some, if any, to complete the sentence: My greatest day in hockey was.... But they took the time and put in the effort and produced thoughtful, intriguing, and entertaining answers. Many more who do not appear on these pages were interviewed and while all had compelling stories to tell, the magic number was 50 and we tried to offer variety, so we say thanks and sorry to those who didn't make it in. In terms of getting to the players and coaches and everyone who was interviewed, it required help and lots of it. Thanks then to my many friends who either provided numbers or e-mail addresses or helped with some of the information gathering. That includes CBC's *Hockey Night in Canada* radio producer Jeff Domet, who would grab the guests for the show and ask that one or two extra questions to get the process rolling. And John Whaley, one of the top sports features producers in the country, as well as Tim Panaccio, one of the top hockey reporters south of the border; fellow Hot Stove member Pierre LeBrun, Dallas columnist Mike Heika, HNIC colleague Elliotte Friedman, NHL public relations folks Gary Meagher, David Keon Jr., and Benny Ercolani, writer Alan Adams, and HNIC radio technical producer Carlos Van Leeuwen for recording so many of the interviews when I took the show hostage (and for passing the files along afterward). Thanks also to old pal Jim Kelley, a Hall of Fame media member, who helped in so many different ways and was absolutely invaluable to the project.

There are few people I have met who are as passionate about our great game as CBC's *Hockey Night in Canada*'s Ron MacLean. But as passionate as he is and as supportive of this book and the last one as he has been, the last thing he needed to do this past summer was find the time to write the foreword for the book. After the grueling playoff run, working virtually every day for two months, then hosting the NHL Awards show and the Queen's Plate, and trying to squeeze a little holiday time around mammoth preparations for hosting the Summer Olympics, he still managed to do it and for that I am very grateful. None of this happens, of course, without the commitment of CBC Sports, from Scott Moore and Joel Darling, and without the superb work of designer Michael Gray, and Linda Pruessen and the folks at Key Porter. As well, thanks to good friend Jim O'Leary, who answered the call to help with the proofing on short notice.

Finally, and this definitely is a case of last but not least, special thanks to Andrew Podnieks, who edited the book. A distinguished hockey author himself, from the first day Andrew came armed with ideas and enthusiasm. That and his deep knowledge of the game and its history, not to mention the anecdotes and direction he provided, were essential and invaluable. It was a real pleasure working with a pro like Andrew, knowing that as a writer, dealing with so many stories and facts and figures, that you have a huge safety net. Like I said, you win as a team and this was quite a team.

Contents

Foreword

In 1989, Scott Morrison, the author of the compilation you now hold in your hands, wrote a book called *The Days Canada Stood Still*. It was the story of the Canada-Russia Summit Series held in 1972.

In the book, he boasted about being allowed to stay home from school on September 28, 1972, to watch Paul Henderson shoot a bear. It was a bear, of course, that was not just big and strong...he was a communist!

Actually, Scott and I are around the same age and we really didn't care about that communist part, and the Soviet Union back then was no more, no less mysterious than any other country in our wide world of sports.

But we did grasp the notion that somehow hockey was our game and the Soviets were set to steal it.

That was the reason we were in a national lock-down back in September 1972. No one moved. Nobody said boo. We were too scared. All of us.

I can't think of any day to top September 28, 1972. I watched that final game in a grade seven classroom in Red Deer, Alberta, and from that day on I understood what's involved in our game.

Paul Henderson had already helped Canada climb back into the series, scoring the winning goals in games six and seven of the eight-game set. And then he came through with the series clincher. Maybe it was a big deal for Canada, the country, but I liked the fact that he knew he had the hot hand, and was ready to play it over and over again.

It's like when the Rimouski Oceanic won the 2000 Memorial Cup. Their coach, Doris Lebonte, said of his star Brad Richards: "He was the scoring leader of the regular season, the playoffs and the Memorial Cup. That shows his teammates and coaches that he'll be there for them all the time. Not sometimes, but always."

I began to skate at the age of four in 1964. I still play hockey three times a week in the winter and on Mondays come summer, and all I ever think about is how cool it is to be there for my teammates and vice-versa. I bring the beer and I forecheck. Of course, the forechecking part comes first. That's my job.

And the truth is I look forward to that ritual more than just about anything in life. I have weekly one-time, perfect days in hockey. Since the days we stood still.

Cheers.
—**Ron MacLean**

Introduction

Like just about any great idea, this one was, well, borrowed. There is no such thing as an original thought, right? Anyway, it was my good friend and colleague Bob Elliott, who is a noted baseball columnist with the *Toronto Sun*, who originally came up with the concept for this book (it was original, at least, to these eyes).

Each Sunday, Bob has a two-page baseball notebook in the *Sun* and one of the items within the package, just a paragraph or two long, was something called My Greatest Day. Bob would quote a baseball player, or manager, or executive talking about his most memorable or greatest day in baseball. It was brief, but a terrific read.

And then the light bulb went on. With the publisher and the CBC pressing for a book idea to follow up CBC's *Hockey Night in Canada's By The Numbers*, which was released in the fall of 2007 and is out again in 2008, the greatest day idea was dusted off.

The next piece of business, of course, was coming up with the stories and trying not to have too many, if any, that were predictable or redundant. That was the big challenge and one that was severely underestimated when the project began. Within these pages you will find the stories of 50 individuals who have had some connection to hockey, telling what their greatest day in hockey was and why.

As you might expect, it took talking with far more than 50 people to come up with those 50 stories, but that was both the project's challenge and its pleasure. Some who had interesting tales didn't make the cut for reasons of space. To them we apologize, although there may be another volume of stories on the horizon, so be patient. To all those who shared their moments, we say thanks.

What was most interesting, though, was discovering the different moments that resonated with folks. In many cases they weren't the most obvious. Take a guy like Wayne Gretzky and think about his Stanley Cup wins, the Canada Cup wins, the scoring titles, the 61 records he held in the NHL at one time, the unbelievable moments that have stockpiled in his hockey life. How do you pick one that is the most special, one that is the greatest day? Well, after some thought, he did, and he chuckled when he saw the amazement on my face. I never would have predicted that story, but I absolutely loved it and understood its appropriateness.

But again, that is the charm. There are a lot of really neat stories from people who obviously have spent time thinking about what has mattered most to them and made huge emotional investments in this great game. In Canada, we all know how much the game matters. For many of us, it began on streets or ponds and continued with 6 a.m. practices in cold rinks, thousands of miles racked up in the car driving from game to game, tournament to tournament. In some cases we were chasing a dream; in others it was simply to have fun. And it carries on from generation to generation.

For me, it is hard to pick that one greatest day, not unlike the folks we talked to for this book. As a player who made it as far as a handful of games in a local Toronto Junior B league as a goalie, it was probably playing in the Quebec pee wee tournament. Our first game was a Saturday night,

8 p.m., and there were close to 10,000 people in Le Colisée. It was as close to playing in the big leagues—Saturday night in Quebec City—as I ever got.

We lost that game in overtime, but the memories remain rich. As a coach, it was back to that same tournament. I was helping a local Toronto team, working with the goaltenders. Prior to our first game, one of the other coaches approached and asked who we were playing. We told him and he said, "Don't unpack your bags." Seems there was a phenom on the team and our chances of winning were slim. Well, our goalie was great that day and we did manage to beat that team. Oh, the phenom was a kid named Mario Lemieux, who scored three goals.

As a journalist, I have been fortunate enough to cover Stanley Cups, Canada Cups, Olympics, Memorial Cups, just about everything big in hockey there is to cover. And to be around to see Gretzky and friends throughout their careers was a thrill.

Few things will ever compare to that final of the 1987 Canada Cup, but winning the Elmer Ferguson award for writing and being honoured by the Hockey Hall of Fame was a pretty great day. And as a parent, well, just seeing my son, Mark, on the ice for the first time and every time is a great day. That is pure Canadiana. We all have our stories and our memories and that is the beauty of it. No matter what level you play, pros or shinny, we all have our greatest day. It might have been Gretzky, in fact, who said: Every day in hockey is a greatest day.

—Scott Morrison
Toronto, August 2008

A Champion After 22 Seasons

For the longest time Dave Andreychuk figured his best moment in hockey would be a toss-up between the night he scored six points in the old Boston Garden while playing for the Buffalo Sabres, which was pretty darn good, or when he played on a line with Doug Gilmour with Toronto in the early 1990s when the Leafs had some memorable playoffs.

The six points, against a fierce division rival in the old barn that was the Garden, was a great night for the player whom teammates called "Andy."

Playing with Gilmour and coming within a disputed non-call (and the greatness of Wayne Gretzky) of perhaps advancing with the Leafs into the Stanley Cup final in 1993 against another legendary Original Six team, the Montreal Canadiens, was another...once he got over that devastating loss, that is.

But then there was that night, some 22 seasons after he had entered the league as a Sabres first-round draft choice, 16th overall, that changed everything.

The Tampa Bay Lightning took a chance on an aging—and never particularly quick—forward who had made stops in Buffalo, Toronto, New Jersey, Boston, and Colorado. Andreychuk was hoping to win the Stanley Cup, and the Lightning were hoping he was the answer to the team's prayers.

That year, the Lightning led the Eastern Conference with 106 points, finishing second overall to Detroit. They beat the New York Islanders in five games in the first round of the playoffs, then swept the Canadiens in the next round before beating Philadelphia in seven games in the Conference finals.

In the Cup finals, the Flames had a 3–2 series lead heading into game six in Calgary, but Martin St. Louis scored 33 seconds into the second overtime to force a seventh game the Lightning would win, 2–1, at home. It was just after the Lightning had won that night that Andreychuk's greatest day was complete.

NHL commissioner Gary Bettman was on the ice. He put his hands on the Cup and called out the words Andreychuk had waited 22 years to hear: "Dave Andreychuk, come and get your Stanley Cup!"

Dave Andreychuk in Buffalo.

Andreychuk holds the Cup high in 2004.

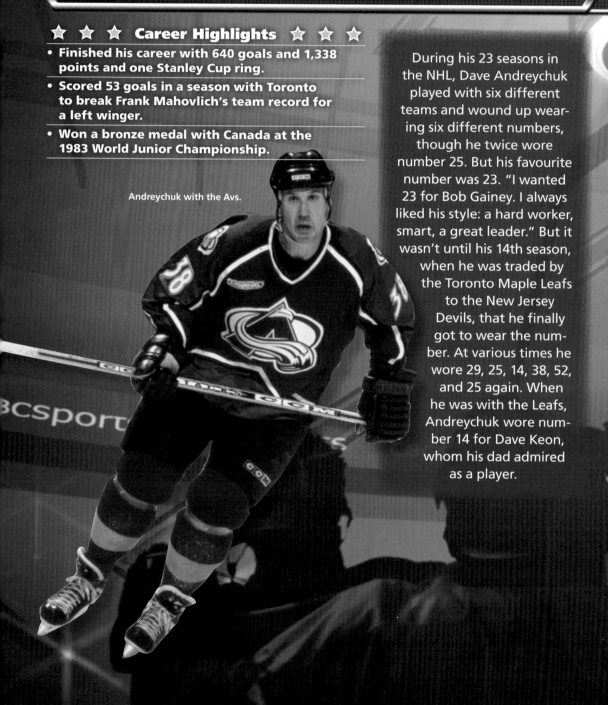

★ ★ ★ Career Highlights ★ ★ ★

- Finished his career with 640 goals and 1,338 points and one Stanley Cup ring.
- Scored 53 goals in a season with Toronto to break Frank Mahovlich's team record for a left winger.
- Won a bronze medal with Canada at the 1983 World Junior Championship.

Andreychuk with the Avs.

During his 23 seasons in the NHL, Dave Andreychuk played with six different teams and wound up wearing six different numbers, though he twice wore number 25. But his favourite number was 23. "I wanted 23 for Bob Gainey. I always liked his style: a hard worker, smart, a great leader." But it wasn't until his 14th season, when he was traded by the Toronto Maple Leafs to the New Jersey Devils, that he finally got to wear the number. At various times he wore 29, 25, 14, 38, 52, and 25 again. When he was with the Leafs, Andreychuk wore number 14 for Dave Keon, whom his dad admired as a player.

Andreychuk, one of the highest-scoring forwards in NHL history and the man who just the year before had seen legendary defenceman (and former teammate) Ray Bourque end his 22-year Cup-less drought, had been summoned to answer a dream.

Ironically, Bourque and Andreychuk had played together in Colorado for a year and not won. Andreychuk moved on in 2000, signing with the Lightning as a free agent, while Bourque finally got his Cup with the Avs. Four springs later, Andy's greatest day arrived.

"I went up there so fast I thought I might bump him [Bettman]. I couldn't wait any longer. I remember lifting it up and it was heavier than I thought, and I swung it up there so high I was afraid it was going to pull me back[ward].

"And then that was it. I had the Cup and I had my teammates all around me and I had my family and a lot of friends in the stands and I thought of all of the guys I had played with and all of the times I thought it might happen and it didn't. Well, it was great. To win it in what I knew was pretty much likely to be my last shot, and to win it as a captain for a team that brought me in to help them become a better team, was just such a satisfying moment. I have a lot of great memories in the game, but that moment, when I was able to lift the Cup, was the most unforgettable night of my career."

Andreychuk had joined the Sabres as a 19-year-old and scored 38 goals in his first full season, 1983–84. Success in the playoffs was rare for the Sabres in those days, but then came a trade to Toronto and the great run in 1993 with the Leafs that ended in disappointment.

He twice scored 50 goals with the Leafs, setting a club record with 53 for a left winger, before he eventually was dealt to New Jersey and started a parade through the NHL before finally winding up in Tampa.

He finished his career after 23 seasons with 640 goals and 1,338 points. And he tied Bourque for the record of most years without winning the Stanley Cup. He was the oldest player, at 40 years and seven months, to play his first finals game.

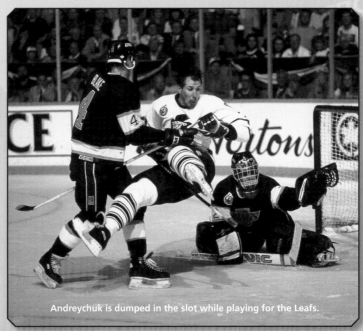

Andreychuk is dumped in the slot while playing for the Leafs.

Hat Trick for Mother's Day

No mother lives for the moment when her son is anointed one of hockey's greatest "shift disturbers."

Matthew Barnaby knew that, but he also knew what his role was in the game he loved so much. To make his way in the National Hockey League, the player teammates called "Bam Bam"(and opponents called names not suitable for print) did, as they say, whatever it took.

His job was to get people off their game. Sometimes he did it with his fists; most often he did it with a piece of stinging commentary, the kind of not-so-polite dialogue for which the NHL is, well, famous.

If Barnaby had a dime for every time he was told he was "gonna pay for that one," he never would have had to draw a salary with Buffalo, Tampa, Pittsburgh, the New York Rangers, Colorado, Chicago, or Dallas, the teams for which he played during his 14-year career.

So you would think that Barnaby's greatest moment in hockey would have been when he aided his team by winning a fight or goading a player into the penalty box or all the other dirty little things that players of his ilk are paid to do.

But that would be wrong. Barnaby's greatest memory in the game came not on a night when he had Eric Lindros chasing him around the rink, or Darcy Tucker boiling with rage in the penalty box. It came on May 10, 1998, in a playoff game against his childhood favourites, the Montreal Canadiens, with his mother, Sandra, watching from a private box at the Marine Midland Arena with the rest of her family and a few close friends.

"I'll never forget that day as long as I live. It was Mother's Day and my mom was in the building, and I had a hat trick."

Okay, lots of NHL players, even a lot whom you wouldn't call "gifted" in the offensive skills department, have had hat tricks. But when you're labeled a fighter (in his first full NHL season Barnaby led the league with 335 penalty minutes) and a pest and you get a chance to show the people who believed in you that you are much more than that, well, it is indeed a special opportunity.

Special in the way a mother sees her son and a son sees the woman who through toil, hardship, and sacrifice did whatever it took maternally so her son could live his dream.

"I knew from the time I scored that first goal early in the game that it was going to be special. I mean, I didn't intend it to be that way, but there's my mom up there [in the stands] and it's Mother's Day and when that first one went in, it just seemed everything was going to go my way. The puck just kept coming to me. In terms of a single hockey game, it was the greatest day of my life.

"My mom did everything for me. She did whatever needed to be done to allow me to play hockey and realize my dream, and to get three goals with her up there with my brothers and everyone who made the trip was just a great, great feeling."

Barnaby wasn't just scoring off pretty plays by his linemates in that second game of the conference semi-finals against the Habs. The first two goals he pretty much made happen through

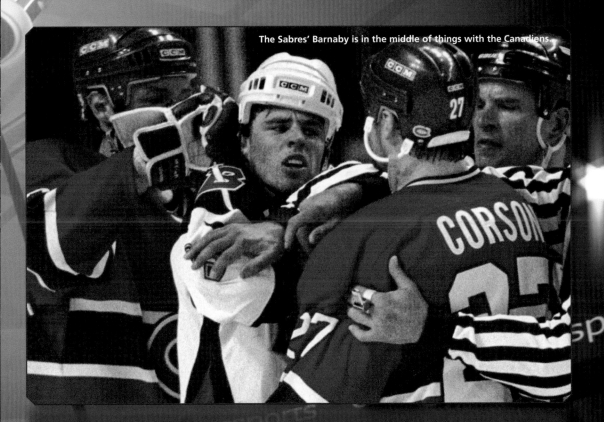

The Sabres' Barnaby is in the middle of things with the Canadiens.

Fighting was a big part of Matthew Barnaby's game, and so was getting under the skin of other players and agitating them like a sore tooth. But Barnaby wasn't above a little showmanship or taking a dare. There were a couple of games when Barnaby would drive an opposing player batty with constant chatter and when the opponent came after him, Barnaby would flash a great big smile. On one of those nights, a playoff game on national television, Barnaby flashed a smile with a twist. On a dare from teammates he had some caps made up with the Sabres logo on them and placed them over his teeth. When he had lured yet another opponent into the penalty box the camera zeroed in on Barnaby for the inevitable smile shot and Barnaby showed some pearly whites but also some gold caps with the Sabres crossed swords. "It was nothing permanent," he said. "It was done as a joke and pretty much on a dare from one of the guys."

Hat Trick for Mother's Day

★ ★ ★ **Career Highlights** ★ ★ ★

- **Best season was 1996–97 with Buffalo. He had 19 goals, 43 points, 249 penalty minutes and was plus-16 in 68 games.**
- **In his first full NHL season he led the league with 335 penalty minutes.**
- **Concussion ended his career after 834 games.**

Barnaby celebrates his hat trick for his mom.

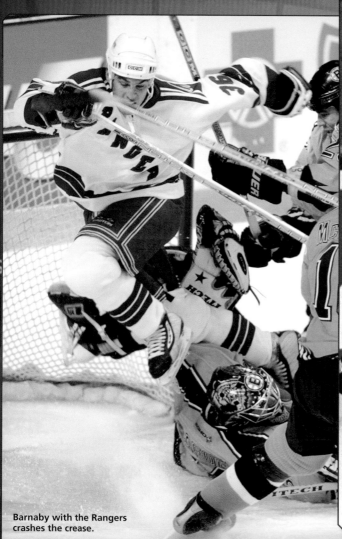

Barnaby with the Rangers crashes the crease.

individual effort, and each time he raised his stick in his mom's direction. After those two goals, he earned an assist, but he still didn't think the unthinkable until Sabres coach Lindy Ruff put him on the ice in the final minutes and his teammates did their level best to set him up for the hat trick in what turned out to be a 6–3 Sabres win en route to a series sweep.

"Look, I would have loved to play for the Stanley Cup, but it didn't happen for me and it doesn't happen for a lot of guys. But when you think of the circumstances, my role on the team, the fact that it was a playoff game against the team I idolized as a kid, and my mother in the building—I mean, how do you top that?"

If you understood the relationship between Barnaby and his mom, well, you'd understand why that was his greatest day. Theirs was a hard life. Matthew was an up-from-the-streets kid, but his mother wouldn't let him go the wrong way. She knew hockey would be the focus of his days growing up, not just a chance to learn skills, and perhaps someday he would realize a dream. It was also a way to keep her son away from trouble. She did what she needed to do to make that dream real.

Barnaby was always an agitator. That's what allowed him to stay in the league for as long as he did. But for all that hard and dirty work, there was the one moment, that one shining moment, when a son was able to perform at the game's highest level and in front of the woman who made it happen.

"That last goal was an empty netter and as soon as I saw it go in I looked up and I could see her up there and she was so happy. I'll never

forget that look on her face and how I felt. That's a feeling I'll carry with me forever, and I think she does, too. I don't think either one of us ever expected something like that."

In his best year, playing for coach Ted Nolan in Buffalo, Barnaby scored 19 goals under the coach he says allowed him the time and the opportunity to showcase his hockey skills over and above what he was largely paid to do. If his mother was the object of his undying affection, Nolan was the father figure that brought out the best in him as both a man and a hockey player.

"Ted made me believe that I could be more than a fighter. He gave me the chance to develop my skills and that's a part of the reason that night happened. He made me believe I could play the game, and I think that showed later in my career. In those other cities [after Buffalo], I averaged about a half a point a game.

"Don't get me wrong; I loved my role— the fighting and the agitating—but I was a good passer and he got me to believe in that part of my game. I played with a lot of great players and I like to think I helped them in that regard, but still that Mother's Day game, that was the greatest day for me."

And does he remember who was in goal for that game?

"I sure do. It was Andy Moog and it was the last game he ever played and I remember that he said afterward that if I could beat him for a hat trick it was time to retire, and he did."

Barnaby scored only seven career playoff goals, all of them that spring and three of them on that greatest Mother's Day of all.

Full-Time NHL Coach

As overnight sensations go, Bruce Boudreau was just 33 years in the making.

Although he was one of the top junior players in Canada and one of the all-time scoring leaders in the American Hockey League, Boudreau managed to play just 141 NHL games over eight seasons with the Toronto Maple Leafs and Chicago Blackhawks. And although he won championships coaching in the minor leagues, it still took 15 seasons before he got the call to the NHL, and even then it was on an interim basis.

"My greatest day? It's any time you are allowed to celebrate a championship, I thought. We won two Memorial Cups when I played junior with the Toronto Marlboros and they were both fabulous. Winning the Calder Cup [in the AHL] was great. But sort of the culmination of all that was getting that phone call at 6:30 in the morning on November 22 [2007] and realizing you are going to be in the National Hockey League. That was probably the most overwhelming feeling that I've had."

The call came from Washington Capitals' general manager George McPhee. He had just fired Glen Hanlon as coach and Boudreau was being called up from the Hershey farm team to take over. Initially, he was called interim coach, but his success was immediate and Boudreau was named the permanent coach on December 26. Merry Christmas, indeed.

At age 52, he finally got both feet in the NHL door.

"The phone call was the most exciting moment because you sit there and you want to pinch yourself. It's 6:30 in the morning and I'm jumping up and down and my wife's going, 'What's going on?'

"When you have been around for 33 years, to sit back and realize you're going to the NHL is quite a thing. Any time I was with the Leafs, it was always on a call-up basis. I told someone I can't wait until the training camp golf tournament because that was the day I was always cut. Usually, teams have their golf tournament at the end of training camp. Usually, when you make the golf tournament, you start the season there. But I was always cut the day before or that day, so I never got to play. So that was always going to be an exciting moment for me, not the idea of the golf, but for what it stands for."

Boudreau was a third-round draft pick of the Leafs in 1975 after he had a record 165-point season with the Marlboros in 1974–75. In the AHL, he scored 316 goals and had 799 points over his career, ranking him 11th all-time. No AHL player had more points than Boudreau in the 1980s. But his lack of size prevented him from finding steady work in the NHL during his 17 years as a player.

He was a playing assistant coach in his final season, and in 1992 he started coaching full-time in the Colonial Hockey League with Muskegon. Sixteen years later, after many winning seasons and a championship win in the East Coast league and in Hershey, the best coach not in the NHL finally made it. Sort of.

"Even this year I was a call up. I was the interim coach, which is typical of my life. And you never take anything for granted. Even till the end, until I heard they were going to offer me a deal,

Bruce Boudreau
with the Jack Adams
Award in 2008.

⭐ ⭐ ⭐ **Career Highlights** ⭐ ⭐ ⭐

- **Won the Jack Adams Award in his debut NHL season.**
- **As head coach, he won the Calder Cup with Hershey in 2006.**
- **As head coach and director of hockey operations for Mississippi (ECHL) he won the 1999 Kelly Cup championship.**

As a standout, high-scoring junior player, Bruce Boudreau twice won the Memorial Cup with the Toronto Marlboros. The first was in 1973, the second two years later. Boudreau made that second even more memorable. It was during a semi-final game against the Sherbrooke Castors, on May 9, 1975, that Boudreau became a scoring machine. During the regular season, Boudreau had scored 68 goals and had a dozen more in the playoffs, but he had struggled offensively in the playoffs and was without a goal, until that night when he scored five power-play goals in a 10–4 victory. Two nights later, the Marlboros overcame a 2–0 deficit and wound up beating the New Westminster Bruins, 7–3, to win the Memorial Cup. "To win two Memorial Cups was fabulous. With the Marlies, we won because we were so, so good. The first final we won 9–1, the second we won 7–3. Any time you win, you think of all the effort you have put into it."

A young Boudreau with his junior team, the Toronto Marlies.

you never know. I'd always ask George, 'my contract in Hershey is good, right?' I never take anything for granted."

Under Boudreau, the Capitals climbed from 30th place in the league, dead last, on U.S. Thanksgiving, to winning the Southeast Division title on the final weekend of the season. The Capitals had a remarkable 37–17–7 record under Boudreau, including 17 come-from-behind victories and a 20–6–7 record in games decided by one goal.

Boudreau was the first coach in NHL history to lead his team from 14th place at mid-season to a playoff berth. It was the 10th straight season that he led his team to the playoffs. For the Capitals, it was the first time they had made the playoffs in four seasons, though the great run ended in a seven-game opening-round loss to the Philadelphia Flyers.

To cap off the storybook year, Boudreau won the Jack Adams Award as the NHL's coach of the year and was also rewarded with a new contract when the season was over.

Boudreau during one of his many call-ups to the Leafs.

"We talked contract on the last day of season. I was pretty sure things were going to be good. I know I have to work so hard to stay up, where I want to stay. I will never forget that day, getting the call. I always dreamed of getting there, but never thought I would. I didn't think anybody would take a chance on me. It's funny, but I had that moment for two hours, when I drove to Washington by myself. I didn't put on any radio and I'm sitting there going, 'Okay, this is what you want, now what are you going to do? That's the whole thing, what are you going to do now?'

"The nervousness of walking into the building and all those thoughts that come into your mind. I remember when I walked in the dressing room [Capitals' defenceman] Brooks Laich looking at me, stunned, like, what are you doing here? Those are moments you sort of just wing by the seat of your pants and hope what you do is good stuff. I learned a lot in those 33 years and I learned a lot in those five months."

Hoisting Stanley on Skates

He is the winningest coach in NHL history. He owns a record nine Stanley Cup rings. He has coached some of the greatest teams in the history of hockey in some of the greatest games played over his 30 years behind the bench. But the day that was Scotty Bowman's greatest was his last.

"I really had to think about it, but I would say my last game. The fact I had made up my mind not to coach the following year. I'm very fortunate because most coaches lose their last game and get fired."

Fittingly, though, Bowman went out a winner. That spring, in 2002, his Detroit Red Wings overcame some considerable bumps on the playoff road and became the first team in NHL history to lose their first two playoff games at home and still win the Stanley Cup, which was the Motor City's third championship under Bowman.

And it was that win that allowed Bowman to slip by legendary Montreal Canadiens' coach Toe Blake with his ninth win and make his career complete in so many different ways.

"If we'd lost, I'm pretty sure I would have held to my word and not come back, but you never know, I suppose. But to be able to go out on a winning note was very special for me. It was just a nice way to do it, without any regrets or doubts."

It was actually mid-winter, during the Olympic break, that Bowman, then 68, decided it was time. "We had that long break and when we re-organized, we took our team to Orlando for a five-day training camp. We allowed the players to bring along their families and I brought two or three of my guys with me. That's when I made up my mind to go. I thought if I could do this in other years, then I am ready to go."

Bowman, a Montreal native, got into coaching after he suffered a head injury playing junior. He was hired by the Canadiens to work in their minor-league system and got his break in the NHL with the expansion St. Louis Blues in 1967. In the first three years of their existence the Blues got to the finals.

Bowman was hired by the Canadiens in 1971 and in his second season won his first Cup. They went on to win four straight from 1976 to 1979, one of the greatest teams in hockey history.

It was after that fourth Cup win that Bowman, who wasn't going to be moving into the front office in Montreal, decided to move on. He accepted the coach and general manager position with the Buffalo Sabres. Under Bowman, the Sabres did well, but he wasn't able to build a champion.

Bowman worked in television for a few years before joining the Pittsburgh Penguins as director of player personnel and added another Stanley Cup ring in 1990–91. He reluctantly returned to coach the following season after the death of coach Bob Johnson, and the Penguins were again champions.

Eventually, Bowman wound up in Detroit, where he reached the finals and lost in 1995. It was the first time the Wings had gotten that far in 29 years. They won their first Cup in 42 years in 1997, sweeping Philadelphia in four games, and repeated the following year with a sweep of Washington.

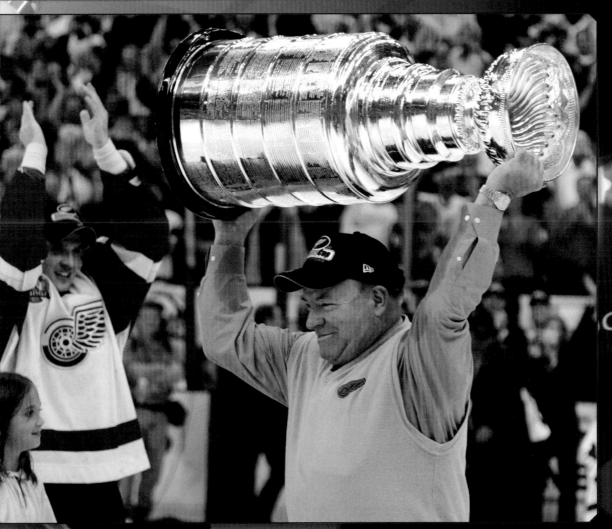

Bowman, on skates, takes Stanley for a lap of the rink.

⭐ ⭐ ⭐ **Career Highlights** ⭐ ⭐ ⭐

- **In 30 years as a coach, never had a losing record when coaching the full season.**
- **Winningest coach in NHL history with 1,244 victories and a .654 winning percentage.**
- **Nine Stanley Cup rings as a coach, two more in management.**

Scotty Bowman

"My other choice for greatest day would be my first Stanley Cup [in 1973 with Montreal]. I had been to the final three times with St. Louis, but we were an expansion team and that was tough. We never won a game in the final. But as a coach winning that first Cup means so much. It's a great feeling when it finally happens. There is a feeling of relief because you never know if you are going to win one. So, it means you can win and that you've really made it. Like the players, it's something you dream about winning but you never know—and it means you've got a little tenure. You get to stay around another year."

In 2002, the Hurricanes upset them at home in the first game of the finals and forced triple overtime in the third game, but in the end the Red Wings prevailed in five games, earning Bowman his ninth championship ring.

"When we won it, it was a close game. Brendan Shanahan scored an empty netter with 45 seconds to go to make it 3–1. I had the trainer all set up. I told him if we win I'm going to put the skates on for the Cup. It was the first time that had happened. With about five seconds to go I slipped off the bench and he had the skates all ready and I put them on.

"At that moment, when I had the Cup, to skate around was great. I wasn't able to do that as a player. But at that moment I felt good obviously because we had won, but I also felt good because I could finally say it was my last game and I was going to go out a winner. I didn't have doubts or second thoughts. If there is any grey area you can't do it, but I felt good about my decision and the accomplishment for our team."

And the symbolism of Bowman wearing skates, carrying the Cup, was a message to his players that he was leaving. "We had a great team, but we had some tough moments that spring, too. We lost the first two at home to Vancouver and we were down 3–2 going into Colorado. But we shut them out in that sixth game, 2–0. I'm not surprised Dominik Hasek listed that as one of his greatest days because that was a big game. But we had a very good team that year. It was nice to be able to go out that way."

Bowman finished his career with 1,244 regular-season victories and 223 more in the playoffs, both records. His Red Wings set a record with 62 wins during the 1995–96 season. He was inducted into the Hockey Hall of Fame as a Builder in 1991. Of the 28 playoffs he was involved in, nine times his teams won the Cup and four times they lost in the final.

Bowman added an 11th Stanley Cup ring in the spring of 2008, as a special consultant to the team and a mentor to coach Mike Babcock. It was the Red Wings' fourth Cup in 11 years and their first in that stretch without Bowman as coach. In the summer of 2008, Bowman moved to Chicago to work as a senior advisor.

Bowman and his mantle of Cup success.

Orr's Leap and Cup Glory

It is arguably the most famous moment in Stanley Cup history and certainly one of the most recognizable photographs in hockey.

It is the image of Bobby Orr, arms raised, flying through the air. A split second earlier, Orr had scored at the 40-second mark of overtime in game four of the 1970 Stanley Cup finals to give the Boston Bruins a 4–3 win over the St. Louis Blues for their first championship in 29 years.

John Bucyk had a front-row seat to witness that bit of history.

"Bobby came across and was tripped by [Blues' defenceman] Noel Picard, but he still managed to put the puck behind Glenn Hall. As he does it and is tripped, Bobby went flying through the air."

The moment was captured on film for the ages by photographers Ray Lussier, Fred Keenan, and Al Ruelle among others. It is forever etched in the memory of Bucyk as his greatest day in hockey.

John Bucyk takes the Cup for a spin in 1970.

"I will always have the memory of Bobby Orr flying through the air after he scored the Stanley Cup winning goal. It was amazing. That was my greatest day. I wasn't on the ice when Bobby scored; I didn't actually see the puck go in. I saw the red light go on and Bobby flying and the first thing I thought was to get on the ice. I was so excited. Everybody cleared the bench and, as you would expect, there was a big pile up on the ice. I still recall everyone piling on Bobby."

That moment might not have happened, either, had Bucyk, who would turn 35 two days later, not scored to send the game into overtime. His goal at 13:28 of the third period tied the score 3–3 to set the stage for Orr's dramatic finish.

"I had a good series myself. At St. Louis in the first game, I got a hat trick and that made me feel good. I had a good playoff [11 goals in 14 games]. After that, the only thing that stood out for me was skating around the Boston Garden with the Stanley Cup. Time was going on and I was getting older and I didn't know how much longer I could play, and it's everybody's dream to get your name on the Stanley Cup."

Bucyk played in the Cup finals in 1956 with Detroit and lost to Montreal. He made it back in 1958 with Boston with the same result.

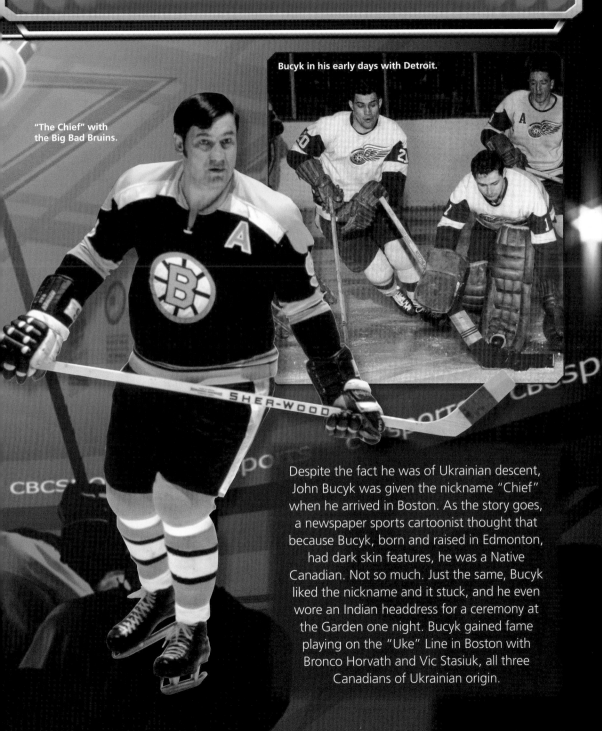

Bucyk in his early days with Detroit.

"The Chief" with the Big Bad Bruins.

Despite the fact he was of Ukrainian descent, John Bucyk was given the nickname "Chief" when he arrived in Boston. As the story goes, a newspaper sports cartoonist thought that because Bucyk, born and raised in Edmonton, had dark skin features, he was a Native Canadian. Not so much. Just the same, Bucyk liked the nickname and it stuck, and he even wore an Indian headdress for a ceremony at the Garden one night. Bucyk gained fame playing on the "Uke" Line in Boston with Bronco Horvath and Vic Stasiuk, all three Canadians of Ukrainian origin.

Orr's Leap and Cup Glory

⭐ ⭐ ⭐ **Career Highlights** ⭐ ⭐ ⭐

- **Played 23 NHL seasons, earning 1,369 points.**
- **Won the Lady Byng Trophy in 1971 and 1974.**
- **Won the Lester Patrick Trophy in 1977.**

Bucyk played his junior hockey with the Edmonton Oil Kings.

"You want that first one because you don't know if it will happen again. That was the first time we did it and it was the first time for the franchise in 29 years, a long time. It made it that much more special. Good for us, and I was happy to be a part of it.

"We ended up winning it again in '72, but right then I knew I got my name on it and that was the most important thing.

"I remember the Cup felt so light. In those days, the captain skated around the building with it. It was after '72, I think, that everybody passed it around and skated with it. Before that it was just the captain who skated around, and then he handed it to the players. So that was pretty special."

Bucyk had been the Bruins' captain in 1966–67, but for a few seasons after that the team had only assistant captains before Bucyk was given the "C" again in 1973. But he was the veteran on the team, the senior assistant, so he received the Cup from league president Clarence Campbell on that historic Mother's Day in 1970.

Bucyk, who played two seasons in Detroit before being traded to Boston with cash for goaltender Terry Sawchuk, had a distinguished career with the Bruins, playing 21 seasons, a club record he shares with Raymond Bourque. Along the way, he played on the famous Uke Line with Bronco Horvath and Vic Stasiuk.

Despite being a punishing checker, the left winger twice won the Lady Byng Trophy as most gentlemanly player, and a year after winning that first Cup he scored 51 goals, at age 35 the oldest player in league history to reach the 50-goal mark. He also became just the fifth player ever to record 100 points in a season.

Bucyk is still the Bruins' all-time scoring leader with 545 goals and holds the club record for playing 418 consecutive games. He finished his career in 1978 with 1,369 points, fourth all-time in the league at the time.

"Chief," as he was nicknamed, retired at age 42, his number 9 retired by the Bruins in 1980, and was inducted into the Hockey Hall of Fame in 1981. He had no shortage of great days during his long career—not bad for a guy who just wanted to get a regular shift in the NHL.

"Winning those Cups was big. And there were a lot of other memorable moments, getting inducted into the Hall of Fame and the sweater retirement. But that first Cup was still the most special. In game four, we all felt we would win, but it was a tight game all the way through, then overtime. We were confident, but it was still scary because things can change pretty quickly. Sure, we were up 3–0 in the series, and we knew it was just a matter of time, but you don't want to wait any longer.

"I'll always remember Bobby flying through the air and then hoisting the Cup."

Bucyk was honoured by the Bruins on February 13, 2007, for his 50 years of service with the team. He has long been admired in Boston for his dedication, his immense talents, and his humility. Indeed, Bucyk's greatest day was as much about the vivid memory of his teammate flying through the air as it was his chance to hoist the Stanley Cup. Always the consummate team player.

A Championship for Guelph

She is the only Canadian hockey player, male or female, ever to captain a national team to two Olympic gold-medal victories. In all, Cassie Campbell has won 21 medals with the national women's team, 17 of them gold, four silver. All were special memories, all great accomplishments on the international stage.

"My greatest day was when we won the Ontario university championships when I was at the University of Guelph in 1995. We were huge underdogs, but we found a way to win."

In that final, Campbell and the Lady Gryphons were playing the powerhouse University of Toronto, winners of the previous seven Ontario Women's Interuniversity Athletic Association championships, including a couple of wins over Guelph. That season, Guelph assembled a heady 12–2–1 record, but the team was still two points behind Toronto during the regular season and few experts gave them much hope of winning in the final.

"I was the only player on our team who was also on the national team. Toronto had seven national team players. The talent they had on hand made them by far the favourites. They should have killed us."

But the Gryphons played as a team, got great goaltending from Jen Dewar and a goal from their captain (Campbell) and somehow fashioned a 3–2 upset victory to earn their first title since 1973–74.

"It was just amazing to see all these girls from small towns improve their games over the course of that season and because of our great coach, Sue Scherer [who had been the first captain of Team Canada at

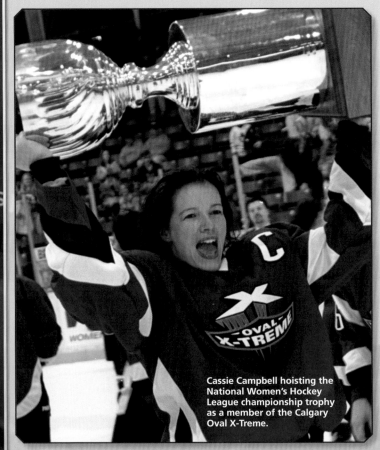

Cassie Campbell hoisting the National Women's Hockey League championship trophy as a member of the Calgary Oval X-Treme.

BCS

Of all the gold Cassie Campbell won during her career, none was more precious than at the 2002 Olympics in Salt Lake City. "That was probably the worst hockey year of my entire career, yet we won. We struggled all year long against the Americans and it was really tough to keep everyone together and believing we could do this." Favourites to win gold in 1998 in Nagano, the Canadians were beaten by the Americans. Leading up to 2002, Canada had lost eight straight games against the U.S., but despite a lopsided number of penalties, including eight straight against Canada at one point, and the struggles to find their game that season, they won the gold-medal game, 3–2. "To win under such adverse conditions and to be such an underdog made that Olympics my favourite. However, by the time we got to the final we had faced so much adversity that the clock could have fallen down at centre ice and we still would have skated around it and won. The officiating really wasn't a big deal to the team in the final because we were so focused at that point. To have everyone's family there at the end to celebrate with us was a really special moment."

Tears of golden joy flow for Campbell and Team Canada teammates.

★ ★ ★ Career Highlights ★ ★ ★

- At the 2006 Winter Olympics in Turin, Italy, Campbell became the only Canadian hockey player, male or female, to captain a national team to two Olympic gold medals.

- In 2007, she was inducted into the Alberta Sports Hall of Fame and was the first female hockey player inducted into Canada's Sports Hall of Fame.

- Scored 32 goals and 68 assists in 157 career games for the national team.

Campbell and Mike Bossy.

Campbell playing for Team Canada.

the inaugural 1990 World Women's Championship] we became the better team despite not having the better talent. We had a lot of good players, but not a lot of stars. But we started with the basics and Sue had us playing our best at the end. I scored a goal in that final game and was named most valuable player, but I brought up Jen Dewar with me. She was unbelievable and she should have won.

"It was a fun year, obviously, as we trained together, went to school together and, of course, we had a lot of fun as a group. It's the first experience I had with a full-time program where you wake up every day and spend every waking moment with your teammates."

But beyond having fun and understanding how a hockey program works, Campbell and her teammates also learned what is the key to victory. "It taught me how hard you have to work to get where you want to go. As much fun as playing for Team Canada is, we sometimes underestimate how much fun and how important our club teams are. We forget how they make us players and how they push us and develop us.

"That championship, for me, really helped to set the table for other success I had, particularly with the national team. I learned so much about what it takes to win. I learned about leadership and that you don't need the best talent to win—you need the 20 best teammates. It's like that for the national team, too. That's when I first realized and understood that it's all about sacrifice and not worrying about who gets the goals and the credit and the glory; it's about wanting to win for each other, as a team. Not many people know about that championship, but I do and I know what it meant to me as a person and as a hockey player."

Campbell, of course, is one of the most famous Canadian female hockey players ever. She became captain of the national team in 2001 and held the title until her retirement in 2006.

She first joined the national team in 1994 as a defenceman, but became a forward four years later. She retired with 32 goals and 68 assists in 157 career games. After retiring, she joined CBC's *Hockey Night in Canada* and, on October 14, 2006, became the first woman to do colour commentating, working a game between the Toronto Maple Leafs and the Calgary Flames. In 2007 she was inducted into Canada's Sports Hall of Fame.

Cassie Campbell

Drafted on a Golf Course

Funny how it works sometimes, but Guy Carbonneau's greatest day in hockey happened on a golf course, not at a rink.

"My greatest day was probably my draft day. It was kind of quiet. I was on a golf course in Chicoutimi—Club de Golf Chicoutimi—which is the city where I played junior hockey. It's not like today when everyone goes to the draft. Back then they held it in a hotel."

Dating back to 1963, the amateur drafts were held either at the Queen Elizabeth or Mount Royal Hotels, or the NHL office, all in Montreal. It was in 1980 that the draft moved to the Montreal Forum. The first draft held outside of Montreal was 1985, at the Convention Centre in Toronto, and after a one-year return to the Forum it started moving around. The 1987 draft was held in Detroit at the Joe Louis Arena.

The 1979 Entry Draft, which was held at the Queen Elizabeth Hotel, was memorable in many ways. Carbonneau was the 44th player out of 126 selected that day in what was one of the best drafts in NHL history. The Montreal Canadiens drafted defenceman Gaston Gingras 27th overall, forward Mats Naslund 37th, and defenceman Craig Levie 43rd.

"When they called me on the golf course and told me I was drafted by the Montreal Canadiens, that made my day. I think it was Claude Ruel who called. I had heard rumours I might end up in Montreal. I had a few calls beforehand. I had somebody from Montreal call and ask me if they drafted me would I be interested.

"I remember that I was kind of anxious that day, but when the call came, believe me, I was happy. Obviously, being French and growing up in Quebec [Sept Iles], Montreal was the team I watched all the time. So it was a big day for me.

"I finished the game after the call—with a big smile on my face. I spent the night with my friends and we had, well, a couple of beers."

Carbonneau, a gifted two-way centre noted mostly for his great defensive skills, had a terrific career with the Canadiens, finally cracking the

Guy Carbonneau

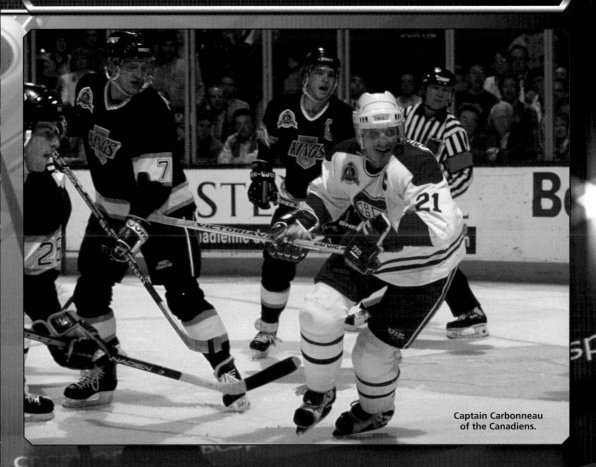

Captain Carbonneau
of the Canadiens.

Like his boss, Bob Gainey, when he was playing for the Montreal Canadiens, centre Guy Carbonneau was one of the top two-way players in the game. During the 1993 Stanley Cup finals, the Canadiens had their hands full trying to stop Los Angeles Kings' star Wayne Gretzky, who had a goal and two assists in a 4–1 victory in game one of the series. Carbonneau went to Habs coach Jacques Demers after the game and asked to be allowed to check Gretzky. Demers agreed, and the Canadiens never lost again. Carbonneau had a profound influence on the series turnaround, too. He was one of the players who noticed Marty McSorley had an illegal curve and requested the stick measurement that led to the power-play goal that forced game two into overtime, which the Habs ultimately won.

Drafted on a Golf Course

★ ★ ★ **Career Highlights** ★ ★ ★

- **Despite having to play against the opposition's best players much of the time, he finished his career plus-186.**

- **Won three Selke Trophies (1988, 1989, and 1992).**

- **Auctioned off the lucky Hermes tie he wore in the 2008 playoffs, which was a gift from his wife, Line, for his 48th birthday. The money was donated to a children's charity.**

Coach Carbonneau rallying his troops.

lineup full-time in 1982. In his 13 seasons with the Habs, Carbonneau had 20 or more goals in a season five times. He won two Stanley Cups with the Canadiens, in 1986 when they beat Calgary in the finals and in 1993, as captain, when they beat Wayne Gretzky and the Los Angeles Kings. Along the way, he won the Selke Trophy as top defensive forward three times.

Carbonneau was traded in 1994 to St. Louis for centre Jim Montgomery, and after a year with the Blues was traded to the Dallas Stars. He won another Stanley Cup in 1999 when the Stars beat Buffalo, and was reunited with old teammate Bob Gainey, who was the Stars' general manager.

"Winning the Cups was special, but without the draft day the Cups wouldn't come. Ask which Cup out of the three I prefer, the first one is the nicest one. That's the one, the memory that first comes to mind. After winning the Cup, sitting down and thinking of the memories of waking up at five-thirty in the morning, your mom driving you to the rink, all those trips by bus, all those injuries you have to overcome, all the training you have to do, the friendships that you made, that's what really kind of comes out after the first Cup win.

"You are so excited you don't remember much of anything after a month. That's why you enjoy the second and third one a little differently. I was able to have fun but take a back seat and really enjoy what it is to win the Stanley Cup."

Carbonneau retired at the age of 40 after Dallas lost to New Jersey in the 2000 finals. He was so popular in Dallas that fans petitioned the Stars to retire his number 21, though it never came to pass. He returned to the Canadiens

in a front-office role and was made part of the coaching staff that same year. After two seasons, he went to work with Gainey in Dallas and eventually started his coaching career. Gainey brought him back to Montreal in 2005 and a year later made him head coach.

But it all started on draft day, August 9, 1979. It was a unique day because it was the latest draft day ever. It was supposed to be June 10, but that year's draft was delayed because of issues of eligibility. That summer the World Hockey Association merged with the NHL, and as part of the agreement there were underage players eligible for the draft. The NHL draft had always been for 20-year-olds, but the rebel WHA challenged the system and had drafted 18-year-olds.

With the merger, the NHL agreed to draft the underage WHA players, and lower the draft age to 19 in 1979 and 18 the following year. Because those WHA kids had played pro, the NHL could no longer call it the Amateur Draft, so it became known as the Entry Draft.

Interestingly, there was one new player who came into the league in the fall of 1979 without being drafted. Part of the WHA's agreement involved keeping two players from each roster, allowing Wayne Gretzky to remain the property of Edmonton.

There was incredible talent that year, with the likes of Rob Ramage, Mike Gartner, Rick Vaive, Craig Hartsburg, Ray Bourque, Brian Propp, Michel Goulet, and Kevin Lowe all being selected in the first round. Later prominent picks included Lindy Ruff, Dale Hunter, Glenn Anderson, Neal Broten, and, four picks after Carbonneau, at 48th overall, an underage forward named Mark Messier.

Bobby Clarke

The First Expansion Cup

Some might say that Bobby Clarke's greatest day and accomplishment was just getting to the NHL. But not Clarke.

The fact that he was diagnosed with diabetes as a kid—and there was a fear that he might never be able to play professional hockey as a result—never stopped him from chasing his dream with the same dogged determination he hunted down an opponent. Others may have had doubts, but not Clarke.

When he was 23, he was named captain of the Philadelphia Flyers, the team that drafted him 17th overall in 1969. At the time, he was the youngest captain in NHL history. If not for the diabetes, he certainly would have been selected higher in the first round of that year's draft, but a lot of teams were scared off by his medical record and ultimately were disappointed they passed him by.

Clarke played for Team Canada in 1972 in the historic Summit Series, also at age 23, and his play had a profound influence on the outcome of the series. Clarke centred an effective two-way line with two Toronto Maple Leafs—hero Paul Henderson and Ron Ellis—a line that scored goals and prevented them. Indeed, it was the only line that remained intact for the full eight games of the series. Clarke played his usual tenacious style and had a further impact on the series when, in the sixth game, he applied a slash to Valeri Kharlamov that left the Soviet star with a fractured ankle, unable to play the seventh game, and ineffective in the finale. It was vintage Clarke—do whatever it takes to win.

Along the way, Clarke led the Flyers, who became known as the Broad Street Bullies in their heyday, to two Stanley Cup victories and became the all-time face of the franchise, winning three Hart Trophies and one Lester Pearson Award. He was twice a first-team all-star and was inducted into the Hockey Hall of Fame in 1987. Clarke carried on for the majority of his post-playing career as a Flyers' executive.

"There were a lot of great days with the Flyers, but my greatest day in hockey was the day we won the first Stanley Cup. It was all I ever dreamed of doing. Like a lot of kids, that's all you ever want to do. Win the Stanley Cup."

In that 1973–74 season, the Flyers finished first in the West Division, but second overall, a point behind the Boston Bruins, who had won the Cup in 1970 and 1972 and would be their opponents in the finals. The Bruins were tough, but they also had an imposing lineup with the likes of Phil Esposito, Bobby Orr, Ken Hodge, and Wayne Cashman, who were the top four scorers in the NHL that season.

"We were really just getting going as a team. We had a lot of young guys—Bill Barber, Rick MacLeish—we were just getting started. And we had Bernie Parent in goal. He was the difference in the series.

"In the first game, Orr scored late in Boston to give them the win [3–2]."

May 19, 1974 Philadelphia Spectrum

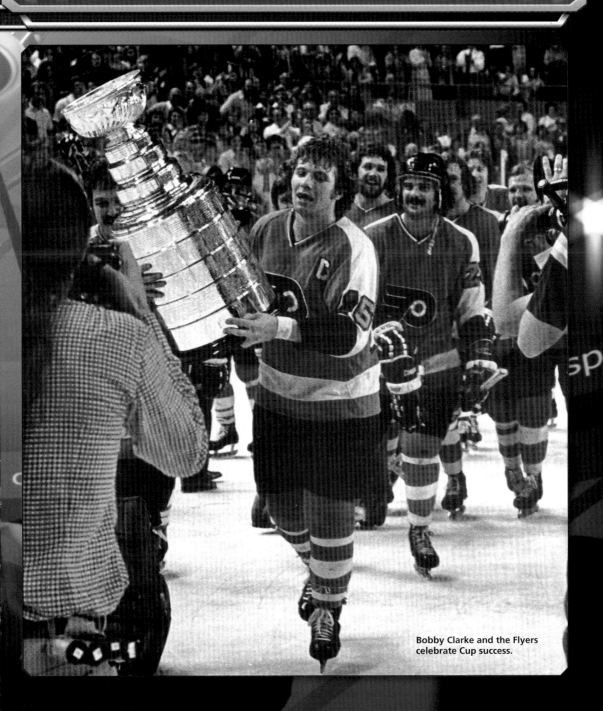

Bobby Clarke and the Flyers celebrate Cup success.

The First Expansion Cup

★ ★ ★ **Career Highlights** ★ ★ ★

- **Won the Hart Trophy three times (1973, 1975, and 1976).**
- **Won the Lester Patrick Award in 1980.**
- **Played 15 NHL seasons, earning 1,210 points.**

He was the last player selected to the Team Canada roster in 1972 for the historic Summit Series with the Soviet Union. But Bobby Clarke quickly became one of the most important players on that team. Lined up between wingers Paul Henderson, who would score the game-winning goal in each of the final three games of the series, and speedy Ron Ellis, Clarke was part of a very reliable checking line that eventually turned into a scoring line. Clarke was terrific in the faceoff circle and good at both ends of the ice, setting up goals while demonstrating responsible defensive play. He will also be remembered in that series for a whack he applied to the ankle of Soviet star Valeri Kharlamov, who had been causing the Canadians grief with his speed and scoring. It was suggested by assistant coach John Ferguson that Kharlamov already had a sore ankle and needed to be taken care of, which Clarke did. He admitted afterward that had he not played with that edge, he never would have made it to the NHL. But he also admitted that he wouldn't have delivered the slash had it been in an NHL game. The Summit Series was much, much bigger.

Bobby Clarke with the Flin Flon Bombers.

Clarke the GM.

In some ways, despite the close score of the opening game, the Flyers were in a hopeless situation. Entering the series the Bruins were 17–0–2 at home against the Flyers and had home-ice advantage.

"In the second game, we finally beat them in the Boston Garden. [Moose] Dupont scored late to tie the game, then we won it in overtime [3–2]. I had a pretty good night. At that point, I felt like were going to win the series."

Clarke had a hand in all three goals that night. It was Clarke who scored the overtime winner, his second goal of the game, depositing a rebound past Bruins' goaltender Gilles Gilbert. He also had an assist on the other Philadelphia goal.

And the team's confidence level rose along with the quality of Parent's play in goal. Over the next four games the Bruins, the highest-scoring team in the NHL (349 regular-season goals), were beaten by the top defensive team. The Flyers won three of the final four games, allowing just three goals in the three wins. In the lone loss, in Boston in game five, they lost 5–1, but bounced back strong to become the first expansion team to win the Stanley Cup after just seven years in the NHL.

"We beat Boston 1–0 in the sixth game in Philly. They were the Big Bad Bruins, with Orr and Esposito and all those guys, a good team. I have never been able to describe in words the feeling you have when you finally win it. It is probably as close to heaven as I'm going to get.

"The '72 [Summit] Series was special. I remember [Montreal Canadiens' great] Serge Savard said winning that series against the Russians was bigger than winning the Stanley Cup. But he also won 10 or so Cups. But, to me,

'72 was something we just kind of stumbled onto, the way the series unfolded and all.

"It was special, but the Stanley Cup is something that starts when you're five years old. It's the dream every kid has when they're playing on the frozen lake or in the driveway. You work hard a lot of days over a lot of years, always dreaming about winning it. All you want to do is carry the Stanley Cup.

"When it happens, it's unbelievable. It's an incredible moment. In some ways, when it happened there was almost a sense of relief. There is ecstasy in winning it, for sure, but there is also a relief because you are in the finals, you are that close, you don't want to come away empty. I made it to the finals eight times as a player and manager and won it twice, the first two times I got there."

Indeed, the Flyers won again the next spring, beating the Buffalo Sabres in six games. The following year they were swept by the powerful Montreal Canadiens.

In 1980, they lost in six games to the next dynasty, the New York Islanders. After retiring in 1984 and moving into management, Clarke and the Flyers lost twice to the great Edmonton Oilers, in 1985 and 1987. A decade later they were swept by Detroit in the 1997 finals. Clarke also got to the finals and lost in 1991 with the Minnesota North Stars during his brief time there as GM. Pittsburgh beat them in four straight games.

"I keep that first Stanley Cup ring hidden away, but I bring it out for the playoffs. Bob Gainey taught me that when we were in Minnesota together, to bring it out in the first round for good luck."

There was a time in his career when Daniel Cleary was a man without a team. But he was never a man without a province and, most importantly, a family.

Cleary is the pride of his native Newfoundland, especially his hometown of Harbour Grace, and the entire province celebrated along with him on the night of June 4, 2008, when the Detroit Red Wings defeated the Pittsburgh Penguins, 3–2, to capture the Stanley Cup in six games.

Cleary became the first Newfoundlander ever to win the big prize. "It is definitely my greatest day. To be honest, my previous greatest day—it was fun being drafted—was in 2007 when we beat Calgary and finally won a playoff round. But this certainly supercedes that. It's so hard to put into words, just amazing. First, I can't believe I did it. It's such a long run; it's not easy to win."

In the case of Cleary, it wasn't easy just getting into the position to win. After a high-scoring

Cleary with the Cup in Newfoundland in the summer of 2008.

junior career with the Belleville Bulls, he was selected 13th overall by the Chicago Blackhawks in 1997. But Cleary played just 41 games for Chicago, scoring four goals, before he was traded to Edmonton, where he played parts of four seasons. He later signed with Phoenix as a free agent. After the lockout in 2005, though, Cleary couldn't find work.

His agent, J.P. Barry, eventually got him a tryout with the Red Wings and he was signed on October 4, 2005. Cleary scored only three goals his first season, but had 20 the next and 20 in 2007–08 despite playing six fewer games because of a broken jaw.

Cleary shares his greatest day with his province's fans.

The Stanley Cup had been to Newfoundland a few times before the summer of 2008. But it was always either on a tour or for a tournament. When Dan Cleary brought it home on June 30 of that summer, it was special. It was the first time a native Newfoundlander had won the Stanley Cup. A total of 26 players from the province have made it to the NHL, yet only one has won. Cleary left the province at age 14 to pursue his dream and had to hit rock bottom before he fought his way back and realized his dream with the Red Wings. As he promised, one of the first stops after the Cup arrived was a visit to a children's hospital. "I think it was my duty to bring it home," he said after arriving with the Cup.

Celebrating with Newfoundland

Daniel Cleary

☆ ☆ ☆ **Career Highlights** ☆ ☆ ☆

- **Selected 13th overall by the Chicago Blackhawks in the 1997 Entry Draft.**

- **Once scored a short-handed penalty shot goal in the playoffs.**

- **Had NHL stops in Chicago, Edmonton, Phoenix, and Detroit and played in Sweden during the lockout.**

Cleary with the Red Wings.

"Hoisting the Cup, getting it handed to me after Dallas Drake, is something I'll never forget. Having the people that I care about the most there to celebrate meant everything. I saw the best of it in junior and then sunk to lows, tough times. I feel so proud to have come all this way back from the bottom when it looked like my career was over."

After NHL commissioner Gary Bettman handed the Cup to Red Wings' captain Nicklas Lidstrom, Lidstrom passed it along to veteran Dallas Drake, who had waited 14 seasons to win. He then passed it to Cleary.

"I had no idea that was going to happen. I kind of had a feeling that Dallas would get it first. He's a veteran guy and such a key component for us and a good person, and he had never won a Cup, so I knew he would get it. But I had no idea I was getting it after him. He just said, 'Go, hold it high; do it for Newfoundland.'

"Drapes [Kris Draper] was kind of directing who was getting what and he said, 'Clearsy, it's your time, go take it.' I'll never forget it. I mean, what a feeling. It's amazing. I had hurt my wrist and I knew it was heavy. I just wanted to make sure I could hoist it up. It's what you dream about.

"When Drapes said this is your moment, when he said it to me, I was thinking about my family, people who were there when times were tough. I thought back to when I didn't have a job and that isn't easy. I knew where my family was sitting in the arena, so right away I went over there and when I lifted it up I said we did it, with some expletives, a couple of swear words in there, but we did it.

"I looked at my wife, Jelena, and I knew my little girl [Elle] was there. I wouldn't have been here without them. For me, personally, it has been a really interesting journey. It hasn't been an easy road, a lot of up and downs. A few years ago I didn't have a job and that right away came back. I go from not having a job, to signing a tryout, then a two-year deal, now a new five-year deal, now a Stanley Cup. It has happened so fast this year; it's been a really exciting year for me."

On June 30, 2008, Cleary took the Cup back to his home province and hometown where he was mobbed by thousands of well-wishers.

"I really wanted the kids of Newfoundland to feel it, to see it, take pictures with it. I wanted to take it to the hospital for the kids, to give them inspiration and hope. Then I took it back to where I grew up and celebrated there, to let the people there realize dreams can come true, that if you work hard good things can happen.

"It's funny, we had dinner—me, Drapes and Malts [Kirk Maltby] always go for dinner—the night before the last game, and Drapes said it's always more fun winning it on the road. I asked why. He said, 'you have the most important people there, the most important people in your life. You get to celebrate it in a tiny room." And he said, 'let's just do it,' and he couldn't have been more right.

"It was so crazy in the room, but we had a really special moment in the back. It was just the players only. We had the Cup, champagne, music, and it was unbelievable. Even the guys who won three or four Cups said we had never done anything like this. That moment I will never forget. When I got to Detroit, I didn't have much chance of making the team. Then I was on the ice for the last second to win the Stanley Cup."

What is in a name? A lot if you are Paul Coffey.

His name, of course, appears four times on the Stanley Cup, three times with the Edmonton Oilers, once with the Pittsburgh Penguins. His name appears three times on the Norris Trophy, given to the best defenceman in the NHL. His name appears throughout the NHL and Oilers' record books and is attached to various Canada Cup championships.

It also appears with his picture in the Hockey Hall of Fame, into which he was inducted in 2004, and it has hung from the rafters of Rexall Place in Edmonton with his retired number 7 since 2005.

"Nothing beats winning the Stanley Cup because that is what you play for, to win and to be the best, but when I think about a special day, I guess a great day, there is one that comes right to my mind. It was just the coolest day and nothing else happens without this day."

It was back in the fall of 1980. Coffey had been selected sixth overall from the Kitchener Rangers that June in the Entry Draft. That fall, the Oilers opened training camp in Jasper, Alberta, and after a week of practising the team returned to Edmonton for the next phase of camp, the exhibition season.

"I will always remember walking into the Oilers' dressing room for the first time and seeing that sweater hanging there with my name on the back. I had no idea I was going to be wearing number 7; that's just a number they gave me. At the start of camp they give you a practice sweater with a different colour and some crazy number.

Paul Coffey avoids a check from Lanny McDonald.

One of the fastest and most graceful skaters in the history of the NHL, Paul Coffey had a secret to his success, though not one that every skater would want to try. Coffey liked a tight fit with his skates and would wear boots that were two to three sizes smaller than his shoes. The laces were tied so tight that after the game he would often have the trainers cut them off. He would also keep the blades on his skate dull, which he said helped him to glide on the ice. Who can argue with success?

Paul Coffey

☆ ☆ ☆ Career Highlights ☆ ☆ ☆

- **Won the Norris Trophy as top defenceman three times (1985, 1986, and 1995).**
- **Was a First or Second Team all-star eight times.**
- **Represented Canada at four Canada Cup and World Cup tournaments.**

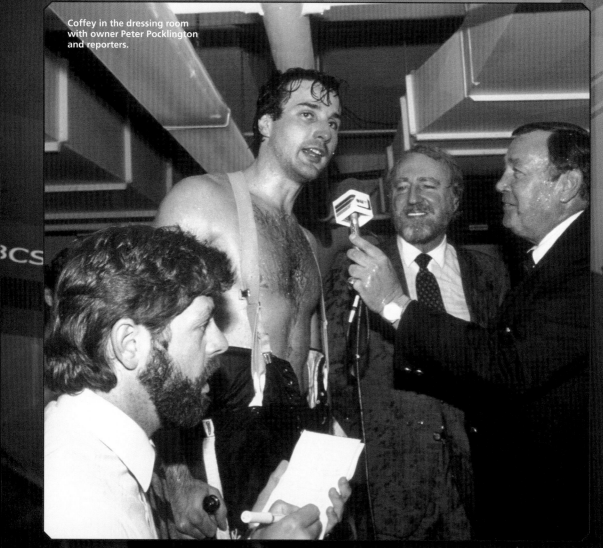

Coffey in the dressing room with owner Peter Pocklington and reporters.

But back at Northlands, for the first exhibition game, it's the actual uniform and I had no idea what number I'd be wearing.

"It was sitting there on the hook and I'm thinking, 'Wow, that's pretty cool. Number 7 and my name on the back. My sweater.' What's going through my mind at the time is that it's a pretty significant number. A cool number. I just suddenly felt some ownership, some importance, that they felt, even though I was an early [draft] pick, that maybe I was going to be a good player and would give me that number right out of the gate. And that's pretty cool."

Numbers are often assigned based on a team's expectations for a player, whether they believe he will make it or not. There was an obvious message for Coffey that day.

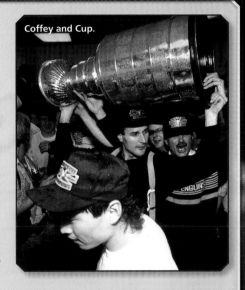
Coffey and Cup.

"Number 7...never in my wildest dreams did I ever think I'd wear 7. In junior I was always 5 or 6 or something like that. In junior, back then, you never had your name on the sweater. I'm not trying to sound egotistical, it's not that, but when you see your name on an NHL sweater, with a number like 7, all of a sudden you really feel like you belong and you've made it.

"I remember that first day, just sitting back and trying to take it all in. You're trying to learn as much as you can and watch. That was back in the day when first-year guys just kept quiet and watched, did what they were told and bought a round of beer and bought another round of beer.... You just did whatever they wanted you to do. It was a cool day."

And the start of many cool days. That first season in Edmonton, with all the great young talent that included Wayne Gretzky and Mark Messier, Coffey had 32 points. The next year, he exploded for 89. In 1984–85, he won the first of his Norris Trophies, finishing with 121 points in the regular season. He set a playoff record for defencemen that spring with 12 goals and 37 points. The following year, he broke Bobby Orr's single-season goal-scoring record, finishing with 48 goals and 138 points, two more goals and one fewer point than Orr had in 1974–75 and 1970–71, respectively.

When it was over, after 21 seasons and stops in nine NHL cities, Coffey had 396 goals, 1,135 assists, and 1,531 regular-season points, with another 59 goals and 137 assists in the playoffs. Those totals ranked him second all-time for defencemen in regular-season scoring and first in the playoffs.

"You think of the highlights and obviously there are the Stanley Cups. Each one is special, but the first one in Edmonton in 1984 was special because it was the first. We were just a bunch of kids, but we knew we were on to something special. But I still remember that first day, walking into that room. I was a kid, just 19 years old, and seeing that sweater with the number 7 and my name seemed pretty cool."

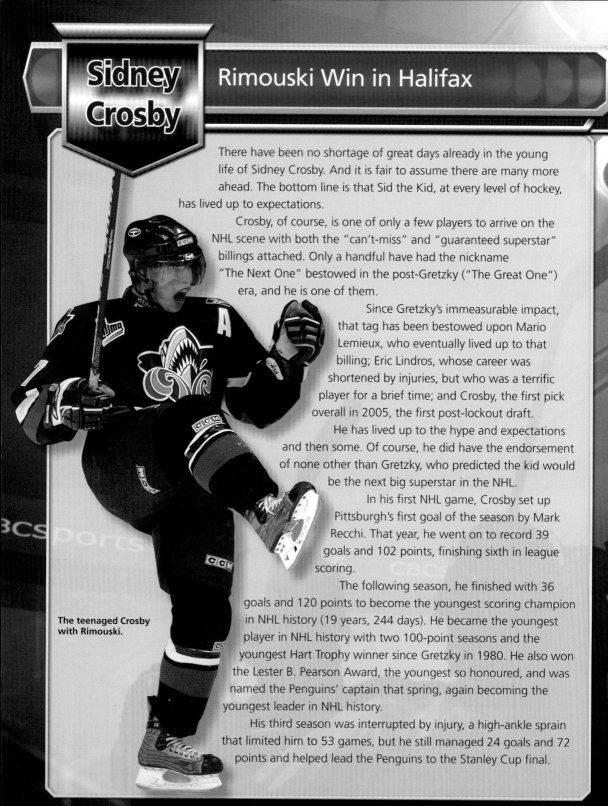

Sidney Crosby

Rimouski Win in Halifax

There have been no shortage of great days already in the young life of Sidney Crosby. And it is fair to assume there are many more ahead. The bottom line is that Sid the Kid, at every level of hockey, has lived up to expectations.

Crosby, of course, is one of only a few players to arrive on the NHL scene with both the "can't-miss" and "guaranteed superstar" billings attached. Only a handful have had the nickname "The Next One" bestowed in the post-Gretzky ("The Great One") era, and he is one of them.

Since Gretzky's immeasurable impact, that tag has been bestowed upon Mario Lemieux, who eventually lived up to that billing; Eric Lindros, whose career was shortened by injuries, but who was a terrific player for a brief time; and Crosby, the first pick overall in 2005, the first post-lockout draft.

He has lived up to the hype and expectations and then some. Of course, he did have the endorsement of none other than Gretzky, who predicted the kid would be the next big superstar in the NHL.

In his first NHL game, Crosby set up Pittsburgh's first goal of the season by Mark Recchi. That year, he went on to record 39 goals and 102 points, finishing sixth in league scoring.

The following season, he finished with 36 goals and 120 points to become the youngest scoring champion in NHL history (19 years, 244 days). He became the youngest player in NHL history with two 100-point seasons and the youngest Hart Trophy winner since Gretzky in 1980. He also won the Lester B. Pearson Award, the youngest so honoured, and was named the Penguins' captain that spring, again becoming the youngest leader in NHL history.

His third season was interrupted by injury, a high-ankle sprain that limited him to 53 games, but he still managed 24 goals and 72 points and helped lead the Penguins to the Stanley Cup final.

The teenaged Crosby with Rimouski.

Sidney Crosby holds
the MVP award after
Rimouski beat Halifax
4-3 to win the QMJHL
championship on his
greatest day in hockey.

- **Had 294 points in his first 213 NHL games.**
- **Had 32 points in 25 career NHL playoff games.**
- **In his first game, he assisted on a Mark Recchi goal in a 5–1 loss to New Jersey.**

Sidney Crosby has always had an attachment to the number 87. As a kid, he grew up idolizing Detroit Red Wings' star Steve Yzerman, who wore number 19. In midget hockey in Dartmouth and with the world junior team, which didn't allow him to wear 87, he wore number 9 because of the legendary Rocket Richard and the fact he grew up a Montreal Canadiens' fan. But once he got to junior hockey in Rimouski he switched to 87. The reason? He was born on August 7, 1987—the eighth month and the seventh day in the 87th year. The numbers 8 and 7 were also prominent in the second contract Crosby signed with the Pittsburgh Penguins, a five-year, $43.5 million deal that averages out to $8.7 million annually.

Crosby at the Winter Classic, January 1, 2008, in Buffalo.

Some observers would strongly suggest, too, that the new arena being built in Pittsburgh would not have happened without the presence of Crosby and that the franchise would not still be in Pittsburgh without him. His impact has been that great.

Prior to arriving in the NHL, the native of Cole Harbour, Nova Scotia, had a terrific junior career with Rimouski Oceanic in the Quebec junior league, the team that selected him first overall in the midget draft.

In his first exhibition game with Rimouski, Crosby had eight points and immediately was given the nickname Darryl, a reference to former Toronto Maple Leafs star Darryl Sittler, who once had 10 points in an NHL game.

In his first regular-season game he had a goal and two assists and went on to lead the Quebec Major Junior Hockey League in scoring with 54 goals and 81 assists in 59 games, finishing as the top rookie and being named player of the year. That year and the next he played for Canada at the World Junior Championships, debuting as a 16-year-old.

In 2004–05, Crosby and Rimouski were both dominant. He had 66 goals and 168 points in just 62 games, leading the Oceanic to 28 consecutive victories to end the season. They won their first seven playoff games to extend the streak to 35 games before finally losing. The Oceanic comfortably advanced to the final, where they played the Halifax Moosehead, eventually sweeping them in four games.

In the final game of that series, on May 10, 2005, Crosby had a goal that sparked a four-goal second period as Rimouski held on for a 4–3 victory and the QMJHL title, winning the President's Cup.

"I would say my greatest day in hockey was winning the President's Cup. It was not an international tournament or the NHL, but I always wanted to play in that league as a kid and I grew up watching the team we beat. My dad had won the same championship."

Troy Crosby was a goaltender with the Verdun Junior Canadiens in 1985, when they won the league title, defeating Chicoutimi in the final in four games. The elder Crosby was drafted 240th overall by the Montreal Canadiens in 1984, the same year that Lemieux was drafted first overall by Pittsburgh, but Troy never played a minute in the NHL.

As Crosby explained: "The guys I won with were an amazing group of guys. The staff was unbelievable and I have life-long friendships with the people I shared that time with. So that, to this point, is something I was very proud to accomplish, especially with such great people."

By winning the President's Cup, the Oceanic advanced to the Memorial Cup in London, but they lost in the final to the host Knights. Losing in the Stanley Cup final in 2008 to Detroit left a similarly empty feeling.

"I don't think anybody likes to lose. Obviously, we've come a long way, but we came [to the final] to win. So it's tough. As a team, we are hungry to take the next step...I haven't won a Stanley Cup."

It took Lemieux until his seventh season to get to the finals, in which the Penguins won. Gretzky played his first final in his fourth year and lost, but that led to four Cup wins in the next five years. Crosby made it to the final in his third season, so the odds are good that an even greater "greatest day" still lies ahead.

Cliff Fletcher

The Flames Give Fletch a Chance

Of all the places Cliff Fletcher thought he might one day become an NHL general manager, well, Atlanta wasn't one of them. The deep south wasn't on anyone's radar, or so it seemed. But the time and the place both proved to be right.

In December 1971, the NHL board of governors convened for their annual meetings in Florida, and out of those meetings they announced a further expansion of the league to 16 teams, adding a new franchise in New York called the Islanders and another in Atlanta, of all places, to be called the Flames. Both would start play in roughly nine months.

"My greatest day in hockey was the day before I was introduced as general manager of the Atlanta Flames. It was my first job as a general manager in '72. It was really an emotional rollercoaster type of day because on one hand I was so elated and ecstatic about getting the opportunity to run my own team and on the other hand all of a sudden the realization set in that I had to make the final decisions, and I broke into a cold sweat for hours.

"I was sitting there remembering back to my time as an assistant general manager [in St. Louis] and running in with these crazy ideas to Scotty [Bowman] of how we could improve our team. But at that moment, that day, realizing that, hey, now you've got to really make the decisions, it was both a very happy day and a very scary day at the same time."

A Montreal native, Fletcher got his start with the Canadiens in the mid-1950s. He was coaching a midget team in Montreal and was hired by the Habs as a scout and to manage their junior team in Verdun. At the time, Frank Selke was general manager of the Habs, and the overseer of their minor-league system was a guy named Sam Pollock, who became GM in 1964 and led the Habs to one Stanley Cup after another.

After what he calls a 10-year apprenticeship in the Montreal organization, a time in which the big team won six Stanley Cups, Fletcher moved to the NHL. He was hired as a scout, then as assistant general manager with the expansion St. Louis Blues in 1966, working under Lynn Patrick and then Bowman. Then came the opportunity in Atlanta.

Cliff Fletcher

Cliff Fletcher is regarded as one of the sharpest men in hockey, having helped build strong teams and organizations in St. Louis, Atlanta, Calgary, and Toronto. And he often did it through trades, which earned him the nickname Trader Cliff. Fletcher wasn't afraid to go big, either. In Calgary, he dealt a prospect named Brett Hull to St. Louis as part of a package to acquire veteran defenceman Rob Ramage and goaltender Rick Wamsley. Fletcher knew he was giving up a potentially great offensive player in Hull, but he felt the potential reward, a Stanley Cup, was worth it. "We knew we had to strengthen ourselves in a couple of areas, on defence and in goal. Ramage helped give us one of the best defences in the league, and Wamsley gave us another top-

Fletcher with his business face.

notch goalie." The Flames won the Stanley Cup the following season, 1989, beating Montreal. A few years later, in Toronto, Fletcher orchestrated one of the biggest trades ever, a 10-player blockbuster. Fletcher traded Gary Leeman, Craig Berube, Michel Petit, Alexander Godynyuk, and Jeff Reese to Calgary for Doug Gilmour, Jamie Macoun, Ric Nattress, Kent Manderville, and Wamsley. Gilmour turned around the Leafs' fortunes and became one of the most popular players in franchise history. A few seasons later, Fletcher dealt away the immensely popular Wendel Clark, along with Sylvain Lefebvre, Landon Wilson, and the 22nd overall pick in the 1994 draft to Quebec for a kid named Mats Sundin, along with Garth Butcher, Todd Warriner and the 10th overall pick in 1994. Sundin, of course, would wind up captain of the Leafs, eventually succeeding Gilmour. Both Gilmour and Clark found their way back to the organization as players and later as executives.

The Flames Give Fletch a Chance

★ ★ ★ **Career Highlights** ☆ ☆ ☆

- **Twice made it to the Stanley Cup finals with Calgary, in 1986 and 1989, the latter his lone victory.**

- **While with Calgary, the Flames won the Presidents' Trophy twice, the Campbell Conference title twice, and the Smythe Division twice.**

- **General manager of Team Canada in the 1981 Canada Cup.**

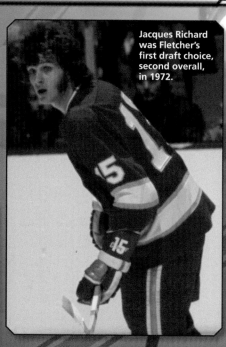

Jacques Richard was Fletcher's first draft choice, second overall, in 1972.

Tom Lysiak, Fletcher's first-round draft choice in 1973.

"It was a funny situation. The two expansion franchises were granted very late, just before Christmas in 1971, and I interviewed in Atlanta a couple of days after New Year's. They actually offered me the job as assistant general manager. I would put the staff together and get everything organized, and in the off season they would bring in a high-profile experienced guy.

"Luckily, I had enough foresight to say no. I turned it down. I said that's not going to work because how can I go out and hire people and put an organization together and then someone else is going to come in and want to do their own thing? Why would people want to come to work for us now, knowing that? They said they wanted to think about it, and three days later they offered me the job as general manager.

"I know I got a lot of help from Clarence Campbell, who was then the president of the NHL, and from Sam Pollock, who was managing the Canadiens. For me, working in the Montreal organization was a great experience. I learned so much, seeing how Sam ran the minor league operation, then after he took over as GM.

"Obviously, we didn't have a lot of time to put the organization together in Atlanta. It was a challenge, but a good one. When we started in St. Louis we had 15 months before our first training camp. After putting the organization together, I remember reading the reviews in the Atlanta paper the morning after our press conference. They noted that I was from Canada but were amazed that I hardly spoke with a trace of a French accent."

In those days, part of the genius of Pollock was his ability to trade aging veterans to expansion teams in return for high draft picks. Quite often, the masterful Pollock fleeced his counterparts, who didn't have much talent to pick from in the expansion drafts and were desperate for marquee players and instant help.

Having been through the start up in St. Louis, which got to the Stanley Cup finals in each of its first three seasons, Fletcher knew what was required to build a good team quickly. It all started in goal. In St. Louis, they had veterans Glenn Hall and Jacques Plante. Fletcher didn't want to build an old, good team in Atlanta, but he knew he required good goaltending.

"I guess the first big deal that I made was with Montreal. We made a pre-draft deal. We acquired a pretty good goaltender, Phil Myre from Montreal, in return for taking a player they wanted me to take as the first pick in the regular phase of the Expansion Draft. So in essence it saved them two players.

"That was the first trade I made as an NHL general manager and it was with Sam Pollock. I had the pockets in my pants sewn tight, believe me, because he was the master."

Fletcher's Flames made the playoffs in their second season and in six of the eight years they were in Atlanta before the franchise was sold and moved to Calgary. The Flames became a powerful team in Alberta and eventually won the Stanley Cup in 1989, defeating the Montreal Canadiens in six games. Fletcher was with the team the whole time.

"To win it back in Montreal, for me personally, was special. And we were the only team other than the Canadiens to win the Stanley Cup in the Forum."

Tony Granato

Sister's Gold

There have been no shortage of highlights in Tony Granato's career. He was a two-time all-star and a second-team All-American at the University of Wisconsin. He was named to the NHL all-rookie team in 1988–89 when he scored 36 goals for the New York Rangers. He played alongside Wayne Gretzky in Los Angeles and went to the Stanley Cup final in 1993. Before his 13-year career was over he played in the 1997 All-Star game and scored 30 goals or more four times.

There were world junior appearances with Team USA, the 1998 Winter Olympics, the 1991 Canada Cup. And he won the Bill Masterton Memorial Trophy in 1997 after he was able to return to play after undergoing surgery to remove an abnormal collection of blood in his brain. It was a pretty good career, all things considered.

He was eventually hired by the Colorado Avalanche as an assistant coach in 2002 and was named head coach a short while later. He took a step back to assistant coach, to continue his development, but in the summer of 2008 he was named head coach again.

But his greatest day in hockey wasn't directly related to anything he did on the ice. "My greatest day in hockey was the day I watched my sister, Cammi, win and receive the first gold medal in the history of the Winter Olympics for women's hockey at the 1998 Winter Olympics in Nagano, Japan. I was watching from home in Los Angeles with my wife, Linda, and our kids. It was a very special moment."

Those Olympics represented the first time women could compete for medals in hockey. Six nations—United States, Canada, Finland, China, Sweden, and Japan—iced teams for the inaugural tournament. All of this, however, was overshadowed by the fact that for the first time in the men's tournament, NHL players, including Wayne Gretzky, were taking part.

On the women's side, Canada was the top seed, based on winning the 1997 World Championship, and the heavy favourite to win gold. The Americans were ranked second. Canada had beaten the Americans in seven of 13 pre-Olympic games and four straight in World Championship gold-medal games dating back to 1990.

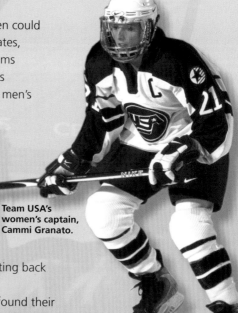

Team USA's women's captain, Cammi Granato.

But in the Olympics, the Canadians never really found their stride and the Americans did. In the round-robin, the Americans bounced back from a 4–1 deficit to hand Canada its first loss, 7–4.

As a rookie with the New York Rangers, Tony Granato scored 36 goals. Not bad for a guy drafted in the sixth round, 120th overall. That season, he was named to the NHL all-rookie team, as one would expect.

But the Rangers, doggedly pursuing the Stanley Cup, traded Granato and his great potential, along with Tomas Sandstrom, to the Los Angeles Kings on January 20, 1990, for star centre Bernie Nicholls. It turned out to be a good deal for both teams. Granato had several excellent 30-goal seasons with the Kings and got to the Stanley Cup final in 1993, a year ahead of the Rangers, while Nicholls was a good player for New York (although he didn't get the Rangers to the promised land).

Tony Granato with the Bill Masterton Trophy.

⭐ ⭐ ⭐ Career Highlights ⭐ ⭐ ⭐

- Won the Masterton Memorial Trophy in 1997.
- Played in the NHL All-Star Game in 1997.
- Finished his career with 248 goals and 492 points.

Tony Granato with the Rangers.

Three days later, the Americans won again, 3–1, giving the U.S.A. its first medal in Olympic hockey since the Miracle on Ice in 1980.

Cammi Granato, part of the national team program from the very first day, was the captain and leader of the American team and is regarded as the greatest U.S. female player ever. She had come a long way, indeed, from playing with brothers Tony, Don, and Robbie in Downers Grove, Illinois, wanting to play for the Chicago Blackhawks, sharing the same dream as the boys, but for the longest time never having a place to live it out.

Said Tony: "When we were kids, my siblings and I always played hockey together. Cammi was always on my team and my two older brothers were the opposing team. Cammi taught me so much about hockey. She has such a passion for the game and resiliency for the game of hockey. She's overcome so many obstacles to play this game, always having a positive attitude, especially when people would tell her that she was playing the wrong sport, and maybe she should have tried figure skating.

"Cammi always taught me—and reminds me—we play for the love of the game, the passion for the game. We love it so much and when the business of hockey starts to get in the way, she always reminds me that it's just a game."

And it was a game Cammi played very well. After becoming the first American woman ever to have a gold medal placed around her neck, she carried the flag for the U.S. team at the closing ceremonies. In May 2008, Granato, who played for 15 years, and Canadians Geraldine Heaney and Angela James became the first women inducted into the International Ice Hockey Hall of Fame.

Cammi Granato celebrates Olympic gold in 1998.

The Last Game, with Walter

Who could have imagined how prophetic a fellow named Peter Pocklington would be on the night of January 26, 1979? Pocklington, the owner of the Edmonton Oilers of the World Hockey Association, decided to throw a birthday party that night for his prized phenom, Wayne Gretzky, who was turning 18.

The pre-game party took place at centre ice at Northlands Coliseum, with the Gretzky family flown in for the occasion and thousands of fans looking on. There was a cake in the shape of his number 99. There was a bottle of champagne, and there was a 21-year personal services contract worth a reported $5 million on the table. The goal, of course, was to keep Gretzky under contract for the duration of his career. "It looks like I'm here for life," Gretzky said that night. "I'm locked up until 1999."

Not quite. It was ironic, however, that 21 seasons later—Pocklington no longer the Oilers' owner, Gretzky no longer playing for the team—that the Great One did, indeed, retire in 1999. They had the term right, just not the team.

It is just as ironic that in a career that was a continuous highlight reel, plentiful with great moments, championships, record-breaking performances, and enough trophies to open a store, that it was Gretzky's very last day as a player that was, in his mind, his greatest.

That day, on the afternoon of April 18, 1999, at Madison Square Garden in New York, Gretzky managed only a single assist, on the only goal his Rangers would score, off the stick of captain Brian Leetch. And Gretzky was sitting on the bench when Jaromir Jagr scored in overtime to give the Pittsburgh Penguins a 2–1 victory. It was the 1,487th regular-season game in Gretzky's career—and his last as a player. It was memorable more for the occasion than the actual performance.

"I would say my last game in New York was my greatest day in hockey. I knew that would stump a few people, but I thought about it a lot. Everything you enjoy about the sport of hockey as a kid, driving to practice with mom [Phyllis] and dad [Walter], driving to the game with mom and dad, looking in the stands and seeing your mom and dad and your friends, that all came together in that last game in New York.

"My dad and I hadn't driven to a rink in years and years, but we drove to the rink together that morning. It was sort of the same conversation on the way to that game as it was when I was eight years old. Make sure you work hard, make sure you backcheck. I'm sitting there going, 'Wow.'

"It was an emotional day for me, to be able to look up into the stands and see my mom and dad, my family and friends. It just brought back sort of all the memories I had as a kid playing hockey and that's why—listen, nothing to compares to winning—but as an emotional day that was the greatest day of my life. It put the ribbon on my career, pulled it all together.

"I knew then there was no difference between playing as an eight-year-old and going to a game and being a professional hockey player at 38 and playing your last game. The feeling was still the same, the excitement was still the same, the relationship with your family was the same,

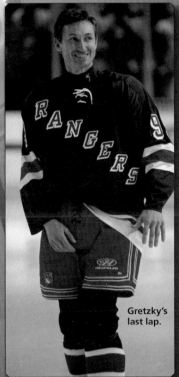

Gretzky's last lap.

When he officially retired on April 18, 1999, predictably Wayne Gretzky was asked what was the greatest performance in his stunning career. There were no shortage of days and moments to pick from, obviously, but one stood out ahead of the rest. "The second game of the 1987 Canada Cup final was the greatest game I ever played in my life. My second greatest game isn't even close."

The date was September 13, 1987. Team Canada had lost the first game in that memorable best-of-three final against the Soviets, 6–5, in Montreal. The series switched to Hamilton two nights later and the pressure was on the Canadians to defend the honour of the country.

"I didn't score a goal that night, but it was the best game I ever played." Gretzky finished that night with five assists, including one on Mario Lemieux's goal at 30:07 of overtime, which gave Canada a thrilling 6–5 victory.

Canada, of course, would rally from a three-goal deficit in the third game to beat the Soviets, again 6–5, with Gretzky setting up Lemieux again for the series-winning goal with just 1:26 remaining in regulation time. For a generation of Canadian hockey fans who couldn't remember, or didn't see, the heroics of Team Canada in the 1972 Summit Series with the Russians, this was the unforgettable series, the greatest ever.

"That series was probably the best hockey I've ever played and you'll never see another like it."

Among other moments that would rate second billing was that third game of the Canada Cup final, as well as the night of May 29, 1993, at Maple Leaf Gardens in Toronto. It was the seventh game of the conference finals when Gretzky scored three times as his Los Angeles Kings beat the Toronto Maple Leafs 5–4 to advance to the Stanley Cup finals against the Montreal Canadiens.

★ ★ ★ Career Highlights ★ ★ ★

- As a 10-year-old he scored 378 goals in atom hockey in Brantford.
- Turned pro in May 1978 at the age of 17 with the Indianapolis Racers of the World Hockey Association.
- In the 1979–80 season, Gretzky won his first of eight consecutive Hart Trophies.

Gretzky with the Cup.

Pre-game ceremonies before Gretzky's final game.

the game itself was the same, the only thing different is I wasn't quite as good as I used to be. That's what I remember most.

"I had no second thoughts that day about retiring. I wasn't scared of retiring from the game of hockey and the practices and everything that goes with hockey. What I knew was that I was completely done with preparing for a season, three or four hours a day of getting ready to be physically ready to go in September. I knew I wasn't mentally ready to do that any more, and that's why I never had any second thoughts.

"The last thing my dad said to me when we got to the rink—I think his exact words were, 'You know, I'd really like to watch you play one more year.' And I was, whoa, that was the most pressure I felt. You know, because he was a fan like everyone else and he was a big fan of mine. He didn't want me to retire, and I think it hurt him more than anyone else. But I was ready. I got nine goals that year. That was it, nine goals. That's what I got the last year.

"On the drive home, my dad was pretty down about it, so he didn't press it again. But I knew it was time and, like I said, I had no regrets. I remember sitting on the bench with 30 seconds left in regulation and [coach] John Muckler called a time out. I'm thinking, I've got 30 seconds to go.... But that day just brought it full circle for me."

As much as Gretzky had hoped to score the magical winning goal, to play the role of hero one last time, on this day it didn't happen. "It was time."

But before it was time, Gretzky established himself, of course, as arguably the greatest of all time. He helped win four Stanley Cup championships in Edmonton and three Canada Cup tournaments for Canada.

He won 10 NHL scoring titles, including seven straight times, and nine Hart Trophies as the NHL's most valuable player, including eight straight years. He held virtually every offensive record possible, at one point a whopping 61 league records overall.

He finished his career with a remarkable 2,857 regular-season points, 1,963 assists, and 894 goals, totals that will likely never be bettered. To wit, Gretzky finished with more assists than the second leading scorer all-time, his idol Gordie Howe, had total points (1,850). And to think he was always told he was too small, too slight to ever make it big!

So many great moments, but one day in a very special way stood out above the rest—April 18, 1999. On that day, NHL commissioner Gary Bettman also announced Gretzky's famous number 99 had been retired league-wide, the first such honour ever bestowed upon a player.

One of the most famous pictures in hockey is of Gretzky skating around the ice at Madison Square Garden after the final game had ended, waving to a tearful but appreciative crowd that included many former teammates and stars of the game, such as Mark Messier, Paul Coffey, and Mario Lemieux, and, of course, his mom and dad.

"My dad uses that picture for more charity events than any other picture. They get $500 to $800 at tournaments and stuff for that picture autographed, so I gave him another 100 signed ones the other day and he was crying." It was, after all, Wayne Gretzky's greatest day in hockey.

Okay, the 2–1 shootout victory over Canada in the 1998 Olympics was a great day for Dominik Hasek. Unforgettable. So, too, was the game a couple of days later when he shut out Russia, 1–0, to give the Czech Republic its first ever Olympic gold medal, cementing Hasek's status as a national hero. The parade in Wenceslas Square two days later before hundreds of thousands of fans completed the celebrations.

And winning the Stanley Cup with the Detroit Red Wings, first in 2002, a five-game victory over Carolina, then again in 2008, the six-game win over Pittsburgh, were both great days, too.

"I cannot put one ahead of the other. They are a little bit different competitions. The Olympics is short, like two weeks. Three games and you're out. You have to beat the best teams in the world and you can win the gold medal. Competing for the Stanley Cup is a long journey. It takes two months to win it and so much can happen. The Olympics in '98 and the Stanley Cup wins in 2002 and 2008 are probably the best accomplishments in my career."

But there is another day that stands out for Hasek, arguably his greatest day in hockey.

"Looking back, probably one game in Detroit meant more for me than any other game. We were down 3–2 in 2002 against Colorado [in the Conference finals]. We went into Colorado and they were supposed to win game six and go on to win the Stanley Cup. I had a great game. I shut them down. We won 2–0, then we took game seven [7–0] at home. That was probably my biggest game, or my most remembered game, in Detroit."

It was another showdown between two of the greatest goaltenders of all-time: Hasek vs. Patrick Roy. Two great goalies, two great egos. At the time, Roy owned four Stanley Cup rings, Hasek none. But in the end it was Hasek who pitched the back-to-back shutouts in games six and seven, just the third time in NHL history that had happened, to put the Red Wings into the finals with the Hurricanes. In game six in Denver, he was brilliant, stopping 24 shots to earn his fourth shutout that spring, tying Terry Sawchuk for the club record.

The 1998 Olympics, of course, were the first time active NHL players were allowed to play for their national teams, as the NHL shut down its regular season for a couple of weeks. In the shootout, Hasek had gotten the better of Roy, who was beaten on the first shot he faced, from Robert Reichel. Roy stopped the next three shooters but didn't have to face the fifth because the game was over.

Hasek with the Czech Republic.

Although the Chicago Blackhawks, who drafted Dominik Hasek, had long had a keen interest in bringing him over from his native Czechoslovakia, it took almost seven years for him to make the jump. And when he did his time in Chicago was brief. Hasek, who had no initial interest in playing in the NHL, was finally convinced to come over by Blackhawks' general manager Bob Pulford, but the goalie wound up playing just 25 regular-season games and six playoff games spread over two seasons. Part of the problem was that Ed Belfour was establishing himself as a great goaltender and there wasn't room

Hasek makes a save during his greatest day shutout performance of May 29, 2002.

for two number-one men in Chicago, so the Blackhawks traded Hasek to the Buffalo Sabres in August 1992 for goalie Stephane Beauregard and Buffalo's fourth-round choice in the 1993 Entry Draft, who turned out to be winger Eric Daze. It turned out to be a great deal for Hasek and the Sabres.

☆ ☆ ☆ Career Highlights ☆ ☆ ☆

- Posted a 389–223–95 career record with Chicago, Buffalo, Detroit, and Ottawa, with 81 shutouts and a career goals-against average of 2.20.

- Tied for sixth on the career list in shutouts and 10th in wins.

- Won his first Vezina Trophy in 1993–94 with a 1.95 goals-against average, the first time a starter had an average less than 2.00 since Philadelphia star Bernie Parent in 1973–74.

Hasek with the Stanley Cup in Detroit in 2002.

Hasek stopped Theoren Fleury, Raymond Bourque, Joe Nieuwendyk, Eric Lindros, and finally Brendan Shanahan. All the while the greatest player of his day, the most prolific scorer in the game, Wayne Gretzky, sat on the Canadian bench, much to the amazement and bemusement of a nation of fans.

"I will never forget the games I played in 1998 in Nagano. When we beat Canada in the shootout and then the final game against Russia. It's something I will remember my whole life. I wasn't surprised Gretzky didn't shoot. They had other players who could score. Not that Wayne couldn't. In my mind he was the greatest playmaker, but the coaches had a different idea."

And the rest is history. Hasek played 16 seasons in the NHL before announcing his retirement, for a second time, in June 2008 at the age of 43. He started his NHL career in Chicago, making a brief appearance in the 1991 finals, before being traded to Buffalo where he had tremendous success in his nine seasons with the Sabres. He won the Vezina Trophy six times and became the first goaltender to win consecutive Hart Trophies, in 1997 and 1998. He took the Sabres to the Stanley Cup finals in 1999, losing to Dallas in six games.

He was dealt to Detroit, won the Cup in 2002 with a record six shutouts, and retired. A year later, he returned to the Red Wings. The second coming was not a great success and he later left and signed with Ottawa in 2004. Hasek played well for the Senators in his one season but got hurt at the 2006 Olympics, had an awkward parting of the ways, and re-signed with Detroit as a free agent in the summer of 2006.

History will remember Hasek as being one of the greatest goaltenders of all time. And one of the more unorthodox. He did whatever it took to get in the way of the puck—flopping, rolling around, charging at shooters, dropping his stick to use his blocker hand to grab loose pucks. He had incredible reflexes—and he got the job done. Hasek finished with 389 wins, 81 shutouts, and a 2.20 goals-against average. Not bad for a guy who never even thought of playing in the NHL, not even after he was drafted 207th overall by the Blackhawks.

"When I was drafted in 1983, I had no idea what it would mean. I remember I was with my friend Frank Musil [who played 15 seasons in the NHL]. I never thought about the NHL. I didn't even pay attention to the draft. I had no idea what it meant, but then I started playing for the national team and I started to think about it. It took a few years to become a starting goalie, but it was worth it."

Although he had a profound influence on how goaltenders played, Hasek doesn't see himself as a pioneer for European goaltenders.

"When I came in 1990 people thought a little bit differently about European goalies. When I came here not many people believed I could play at the elite level. I'm not sure I was a pioneer. Guys like Jiri Crha and Pelle Lindbergh, who was the first European to win the Vezina, were before me. When I started to play here, I wasn't thinking about who you are or what you are. I just went onto the ice and did my best."

Paul Henderson

Game Seven Heroics

"Henderson has scored for Canada." Those five words, spoken by the late play-by-play-legend Foster Hewitt, evoke for Canadian fans a sense of time and place that remains an integral part of the country's hockey history.

And if any player's greatest day in hockey was ever etched in stone for him, it would be Paul Henderson, who scored the historic goal with 34 seconds remaining in the eighth and final game of the Summit Series, to give Team Canada a 6–5 victory and the series win.

This was a series, of course, that Canada simply couldn't lose. It was the first time Canada's professionals had played the best the Soviet Union had to offer. It was a time when the Russians were still very much a mystery, on and off ice, and the country's politics and sports were viewed as the enemy.

Losing simply wasn't an option, but losing was looking very much like a real proposition, especially after the Canadians were an unimpressive 1–2–1 in the first four games in Canada, and a nation's fans became increasingly frustrated.

Matters became worse after the Canadians blew a lead, which Henderson had given them with a two-goal effort, only to lose again in the fifth game in Moscow. After that, there was no margin for error. Henderson scored the game-winning goal in each of the final three games as a nation stood still, engrossed in the drama that was unfolding, the outcome in doubt until Henderson scored for Canada with 34 seconds remaining in the series.

For all the monumental importance of that series-winning goal, however, Henderson took greater satisfaction from the winning goal he scored in the previous game. With the score tied 3–3, a tie not of much use to Canada, there was a faceoff in the Canadian zone with less than three minutes to play. The draw was won by centre Bobby Clarke, who along with Henderson and Ron Ellis formed one of Canada's best lines, the only line to play the entire series together.

Eventually, the puck found its way to defenceman Serge Savard, who hit a streaking Henderson with a long, lead pass at centre ice. Henderson took the puck and attempted to deke past both Soviet defencemen as he rushed into the zone. As he did, he was hit. He pushed the puck around one of the defencemen, eased by, and then, while falling, fired a shot between the arm and body of goaltender Vladislav Tretiak at 17:54. Canada hung on to win 4–3 to set the up the historic eighth game.

"From a personal satisfaction standpoint, the winning goal in the seventh game was my greatest moment. In terms of individual effort. I went through half the team to score. I told my wife, Eleanor, at the time that I could die a happy man if I never scored again because I will never score a bigger goal than that one.

"Well, I guess I should have said I would never score a prettier goal because I guess I scored a slightly bigger one in game eight. But that goal was one I always remember as being my best in terms of satisfaction and being a beautiful goal and individual effort.

Henderson and teammates outside the Hockey Hall of Fame's dedication to the Team of the Century.

We all know the impact The Goal had on the hockey world. For Team Canada, the winning goal Paul Henderson scored in the eighth and final game of the Summit Series saved the hockey-playing reputation of a nation. It defended Canada's honour and prevented what would have been regarded by some as a huge embarrassment. But Henderson likes to tell the story of the impact that series and that goal had on the lives of one particular couple. "I met a couple after I had returned home and was on a trip out west. They told me how they had split in 1972 and were going to get a divorce. The husband wound up coming back to the house one day to pick up a few things and say his goodbyes and the final game was on television. So they sat down and watched the third period together. When I scored that goal, they both jumped up and started yelling and they looked at each other and realized they still loved each other. They wrote me a letter saying, 'You not only saved our country, but you saved our marriage, too.'"

★ ★ ★ Career Highlights ★ ★ ★

- Seven goals and three assists in the Summit Series.

- Scored 20 goals or more seven times in the NHL, his career-high 38 with Toronto in 1971–72.

- In 1997, on the 25th anniversary of The Goal in Moscow, a stamp was issued by Canada Post and a silver coin by the Royal Canadian Mint.

Henderson doesn't beat Tretiak here as he does later in the series when it counted the most.

"That goal was special. We were desperate. If we don't win that game, then the next game, the goal doesn't matter. We would have been known and remembered as being the biggest losers of all time. If I don't score that goal, in the final couple of minutes, the rest means nothing.

"I knew it was going to be my last shift in the game probably. I remember saying to myself, 'Well, if you're going to score and win this thing you had better do it now because you're not going to get another chance.'

"I just took off with the puck and I can remember it like it was happening in slow motion. I moved around the defence and I was falling as I shot, but I knew I had to put it up top to score. Talk about a moment of incredible satisfaction. I remember it vividly."

The eighth game, September 28, 1972, had obvious drama. After two periods, the Canadians found themselves trailing the Russians, 5–3, and defeat seemed unavoidable.

"It's funny. In that last game we all thought we were going to win. Even going into the third period we were frustrated, but we were confident. We had started to play better as the series went along. We knew if we could get one early, we'd have a chance. The thought of losing just didn't fit in the equation."

Phil Esposito scored the key early goal at 2:27 to further fuel the team's confidence. At 12:56 he helped to set up the tying goal by Yvon Cournoyer, though the goal light didn't go on and a major controversy ensued. Eventually the goal was counted, setting the stage for Henderson and one of the most memorable moments in Canadian sports history.

In the final minute, though, the Canadians had Esposito, Cournoyer, and Pete Mahovlich on the ice. They were tired, but couldn't get off for a change. As the puck moved up the ice, Cournoyer thought about coming off but didn't. Esposito had the puck and Mahovlich heard his name called from the bench. It was Henderson doing the yelling.

"I still don't know why I did it, why I called him off, and I'd like to know the answer. I never did it before and I never did it again. But something told me I had to get on the ice. So I called Pete off. Thank goodness he thought it was the coach and listened."

The Soviets had the puck behind their goal and threw it around the boards, but because Cournoyer didn't leave the ice he was able to reach it. He tried to hit Henderson, who was streaking into the zone down the left side, with a pass, but missed. Henderson tried to reach back for the pass, fell and slid heavily into the end boards.

The puck came out from the corner, but the Soviet defence fumbled it. Esposito snapped a shot but Tretiak made the save. The rebound went to Henderson. He slid it along the ice but again Tretiak made the stop. The rebound came right back to Henderson, though, and he flipped it past the fallen goaltender.

"That last goal, the winning goal, was a garbage goal. I mean, I was just in front of the net and flipped it by Tretiak. It was a big goal, obviously, but it wasn't a pretty goal, not like the goal I scored in the seventh game. But everyone has been looking at that garbage goal for 36 years. It still drives me crazy."

Henderson has scored for Canada.

Troops Play with Alumni

In his official biography, General Rick Hillier writes that he "enjoys most recreational pursuits but, in particular, runs slowly, plays hockey poorly, and golfs not well at all."

But he is a good soldier, which apart from sharing most every Canadian kid's dream of being a hockey player, is what the native of Campbellton, Newfoundland, always wanted to be. From the age of eight he wrote recruiters trying to join the Canadian Army. At 17, he finally did.

And when it comes to hockey, Canada's former top soldier is still an avid fan, particularly of the Toronto Maple Leafs, his favourite team. When the Stanley Cup made its first visit to the war zone in southern Afghanistan in 2007, Defence Minister Peter MacKay joked that, "it's a shame the Taliban are closer to the Stanley Cup than the Maple Leafs." It was the second visit of the Stanley Cup, though, that produced Hillier's greatest day in hockey in a very unlikely setting.

Hillier in his ball hockey fatigues.

"No question, my greatest day was 20 March, 2008. We had a Team Canada with us, made up of a variety of former NHL players like Bobby Probert, Mark Napier, Stu Grimson, Mike Pelyk, Dave Hutchison, Tony Currie, Mike Gartner, and a few others. We had that team playing our Task Force Afghanistan team, which is our Canadian soldiers, and I got to play alongside them. My wife, Joyce, was the honourary team captain for Team Canada. It was a special day. And we had the Stanley Cup there. Soldiers lined up for hours to have their picture taken with it and to meet with the players."

As part of the visit, the NHL alumni, or Team Canada as they were called, played Team Kandahar, the Canadian soldiers, in front of a thousand or so spectators, in 40-degree Celsius heat, on a rink military engineers built a few years earlier. How Canadian that right beside the rink was a Tim Hortons coffee shop.

"To go on the ball hockey rink, in front of the Tim Hortons, in southern Afghanistan, and watch our young soldiers play those NHL heroes of theirs in the middle of a war zone and realize that they had come half way around the world just to do that, to show their appreciation, was one of

NHL alumnus Mark Napier wheels as Hillier gives chase.

On July 1, 2008, Canadian General Rick Hillier ended his 35 years of service to his country as a soldier. Fittingly, he did it on the country's 141st birthday— Canada Day. In Newfoundland, where Hillier is from, that day is also known as Memorial Day. And this one marked the 92nd anniversary of the opening day of the Battle of the Somme in 1916, when all but 68 of the 801 men of the 1st Newfoundland Regiment were lost during a massive British assault against the Germans.

⭐ ⭐ ⭐ **Career Highlights** ⭐ ⭐ ⭐

- On May 30, 2003, Hillier assumed the duties of Chief of the Land Staff.
- Says he enjoys most recreational activities, but runs slowly, plays hockey poorly, and golfs not well at all.
- Graduated from Memorial University of Newfoundland in 1975 with a Bachelor of Science degree.

Hillier with Mike Bolt, Keeper of the Stanley Cup.

the most incredibly inspiring and moving things that I have ever been a part of in my life. It was incredible.

"We had Blue Rodeo sing 'O Canada' to start the game. It was an absolutely phenomenal event. To be with our soldiers on the bench, all wearing their Canadian Forces hockey sweaters, just watching them be excited by the opportunity to play these guys they had watched on television and cheered for so much, and realizing how far they had come to do that for them was one of the most incredibly inspiring moments I have been a part of. It meant so much for these soldiers, who are a long way from home, working very hard."

And even for a battle-hardened general it was fun to be part of, taking a few shifts and wearing the captain's "C" proudly on his chest. "They beat us 9–2 or something, but it didn't matter. It was just a truly inspirational day. We're Canadians and hockey is our passion and for our soldiers to have a day like that was incredibly inspiring."

Team Canada played a United States team the next day and won handily, 8–2. Before returning home, Team Canada took on the forces "all-star" team, which had been whittled down from 70 players in the initial tryouts. The NHLers won that game, 5–1. Of course, the scores were not the point of the games.

Hillier stepped down as Canada's Chief of Defence Staff in the summer of 2008, after three years on the job, and accepted the position of Chancellor at his alma mater, Memorial University, in St. John's, Newfoundland.

The troops pose for a group shot after the game.

He played 34 professional seasons stretched over six decades and was one of the greatest players of all time. The nickname Mr. Hockey says it all.

He won four Stanley Cups with the Detroit Red Wings (1950, 1952, 1954, and 1955), leading them to a record seven straight first-place finishes. Six times he won the Hart Trophy. Six times he led the league in scoring.

Including playoffs, he appeared in a staggering 1,924 NHL games, scoring 869 goals and 2,010 points. He is also the only father to play with his sons in an NHL game. But the greatest day in the career of Gordie Howe came way back in his 13th NHL season.

The occasion was Gordie Howe Night at the Olympia in Detroit. That night the Red Wings were playing the Boston Bruins. During the first intermission Howe received a handsome collection of gifts, including a new station wagon with his initials and the number 9 on the license plate: GH-9000. The car was driven out to centre

Howe during the 1979–80 season, age 52.

ice wrapped in paper. When Howe tore away the wrapping, he was surprised to find his mother and father, Katherine and Ab Howe, sitting in the front seat.

Here's what he said that night as he tried unsuccessfully to fight back tears: "This is the greatest day of my life since I came to this wonderful city of Detroit."

Here's what he said, unprompted, in the summer of 2008, almost half a century later: "That was my greatest day, the day my mom and dad saw me for the first time at the Olympia. It was the first time they had ever seen me play in a big-league arena. I don't think I got a goal, but it sure added more feeling."

Howe's mom had actually seen the Red Wings play in 1950 when she came to Detroit after Howe had suffered a fractured skull and required surgery to relieve the pressure on the brain. But neither parent had seen Howe play in the NHL except on television. That day, Howe actually managed an assist in a 2–2

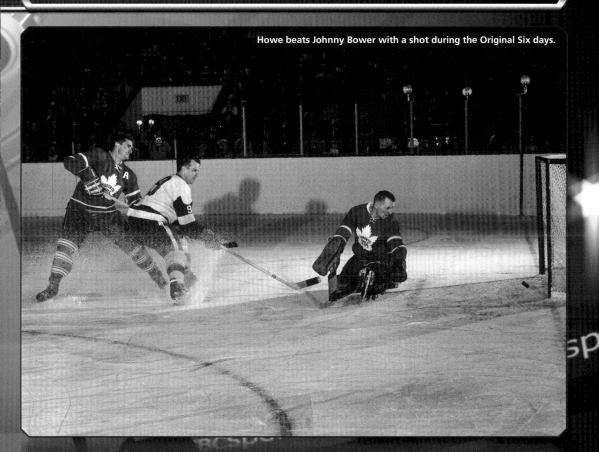

Howe beats Johnny Bower with a shot during the Original Six days.

In hockey, there is a phenomenon, or occurrence, known as the Gordie Howe hat trick. It's when a player scores a goal, earns an assist, and engages in a fight all in the same game, and it is named after the hockey legend who was a great scorer, gifted playmaker, and tough as nails. Many players have had the Gordie Howe hat trick, and many have done it multiple times. The stats departments of several NHL teams actually keep track of this stat and *The Hockey News* once reported that Brendan Shanahan was the all-time, unofficial leader with nine. But as unlikely as it might seem, the man himself apparently did it just once according to those who keep track of such information. Howe always believed he had more, as you would expect, but the stats freaks have found only one on record, December 22, 1955, against the Boston Bruins.

A Surprise Visit from Mom and Dad

☆ ☆ ☆ **Career Highlights** ☆ ☆ ☆

- Known, simply, as Mr. Hockey.
- Played 34 pro seasons from 1945 to 1997.
- Finished in the top 5 in NHL scoring for 20 straight seasons.

The ageless Mr. Hockey.

tie with the Bruins and was feted with many other gifts, including golf clubs, a trip to Miami and a diamond ring from his teammates.

"The best gift was the presence of my mom and dad," he was quoted as saying that day in the Olympia. "Don't mind the odd tear. It's a long way from Saskatoon. I want to thank you for the biggest thrill in my life."

Born in Floral, Saskatchewan, in 1928, Howe debuted with the Red Wings in 1946 at the age of 18 and scored on Toronto's Turk Broda in his first game. His signing bonus that first year was a Red Wings jacket.

With linemates Sid Abel and Ted Lindsay, Howe was one-third of the great Production Line. Howe went on, of course, to become the NHL's all-time scoring leader until Wayne Gretzky, who idolized Howe, came along and started erasing his records. For 20 straight seasons, Howe finished in the top five in scoring.

Howe actually retired after the 1970–71 season because of a chronic wrist problem but decided to return to the game in 1973 with the Houston Aeros of the World Hockey Association because of the opportunity to play with his sons, Mark and Marty. "That first game I played with Mark and Marty was my other greatest day. It was pretty special to play with the boys."

Howe and his successor, Wayne Gretzky.

Howe returned to the NHL in 1979 with the Hartford Whalers, along with Mark and Marty, to become the first-ever father-son combination in NHL history. He retired again in 1980, at the age of 52, having played all 80 games of that final season, scoring 15 goals and 41 points. The highlight of the year, though, came at the All-Star Game at the new Joe Louis Arena in Detroit when he received the loudest and longest ovation in the history of the All-Star Game.

In 1997 he made a one-game appearance with the Detroit Vipers of the International Hockey League. Howe was 69 at the time and became the only player to play in six decades. In the end, Mr. Hockey played 26 NHL seasons and six more in the WHA. He had a combined 1,071 goals, 1,518 assists, and 2,589 points. He was inducted into the Hockey Hall of Fame in 1972.

Kelly Hrudey

Making It to the Big Tent

Although he played in a Stanley Cup final on the same team as Wayne Gretzky, and played in one of the longest games ever in playoff history during his 15 distinguished years in the NHL, goaltender Kelly Hrudey's greatest day was at the start of that run.

It is a day every player alternately dreads and dreams of. It is the last day of the exhibition season, the day of the final cuts. It is a great day if you make it, and an excruciating one if you don't.

A second-round draft choice, 38th overall, of the New York Islanders in 1980, Hrudey had seen that day from both sides. "There's no question what my greatest day was. It was the day I made the New York Islanders back in 1983. I remember the day very clearly because it started out like the two previous years when I went to training camp.

"When you're near the end of camp and they've already sent guys down to minors, there's a small group remaining and I was in that small group a couple of times prior. On this day, we're all waiting outside [Islanders' general manager] Bill Torrey's office and each guy files in and each guy files out with the same wording that you're going down to the minors, have a good year and work on this and that and so on.

"So the third year, there is the same group, about six or seven of us, all of them my friends whom I had played with in the minors. Each one was going in and coming out disappointed, of course, that they hadn't made the Islanders and they hadn't made their dream of playing in the National Hockey League.

"I was the last to go in and much to my delight and surprise Mr. Torrey said I had made the Islanders. I was over-the-moon excited, as you would expect. But I couldn't show that emotion when I came out of the room because there were all my disappointed friends—guys like Kevin Divine, Darcy Regier, Monty Trottier, who was my roommate for two years in Indianapolis. In the minors, when you're together, you're together. You spend all your time together and have a really special relationship.

Kelly Hrudey with the Islanders soon after making the team.

Kelly Hrudey makes a save on Toronto's Peter Zezel.

Most people know who scored the winning goal in the longest game in New York Islanders' club history. That was the game that eventually became known as the Easter Epic, game seven of the 1987 division final, when the Islanders defeated the Washington Capitals, 3–2. The winning goal was scored a few minutes before 2 a.m. Eastern time, on Easter morning, almost seven hours after puck drop. The goal came after 68:47 of overtime and was scored by Pat LaFontaine. And the winning goaltender? Kelly Hrudey, who made a playoff record 73 saves. "As the night went on, I didn't even know the velocity of the shots anymore. I was too tired to have any emotion. It gets to the point where your body doesn't feel anything and your mind plays the game. It was a once-in-a-lifetime thing."

★ ★ ★ **Career Highlights** ★ ★ ★

- Played 15 seasons with the Islanders, Los Angeles, and San Jose, finishing with a 271–265–88 record, a 3.43 goals-against average and 17 shutouts.

- In his first year of junior in Medicine Hat, he had a 12–34–7 record and a 6.17 goals against average.

- Hrudey's on-air segment "Behind the Mask" became a regular feature on CBC's *Hockey Night in Canada* in the 1999 playoffs.

Hrudey with Los Angeles.

"I didn't want to break that by coming across as some arrogant idiot now that all of a sudden I was getting a chance in the NHL. So I tried to manipulate the words a little bit, something to the effect of, 'Yeah, I'm here just for a little bit. They don't know what's going to happen,' and so on, trying to make it sound not so exciting. But inside I was going absolutely nuts.

"I remember I had to stay around for something and I had a moment alone. I was walking from the Nassau Coliseum to the Marriott Hotel across the parking lot and it was right about the time of those *Rocky* movies. Well, I was Rocky running up those stairs. There weren't any stairs, but I was running and yelling and swearing, my arms in the air, because like every kid you grow up hoping but never really expect to be a professional hockey player.

"First thing I did was call home. But back in the day there were no cell phones, so it took longer than expected to get a hold of my parents. I was so naïve back then. I had no idea what I was getting into, what life would be like.

"I didn't start playing hockey until I was 12 years old, and all of a sudden 10 years later I'm playing in the NHL. The first-ever jersey I bought as a kid was the New York Islanders because Clark Gillies was one of my many heroes."

Incredibly, Hrudey didn't start playing until he was 12 because, simply, he had no desire to play organized hockey. "When I was 11, I mentioned to my mom and dad that I wanted to play. My dad gave me some great advice. He said wait a year and learn how to skate, and then you can play.

"I had skated when I was younger but had stopped for a few years, but then I skated virtually every day I could and in Edmonton back then it was colder and easier to do. I played a lot of ball hockey but didn't have a desire to play organized hockey until I was 11. I actually started in goal, too, because of the road hockey.

"A buddy and I were discussing what position I should play when I started and his dad overheard us. He said, 'I don't want to influence you, but I've seen you playing ball hockey and you seem to stop more shots than the rest of the kids.' So I figured why not, I'll give it a try."

Hrudey advanced quickly and played his junior hockey in Medicine Hat, attending his first training camp with the Islanders in 1980.

"We had seven goalies at camp and I was clearly number six or seven. I was a second-round pick. You look at the depth chart and think the NHL is light years away. But that year at the end of camp they got rid of a couple of guys. I ended up playing two years in the minors in Indianapolis and won two championships. They didn't rush me, and that was a good thing."

When he finally made the Islanders, they still didn't rush him. He was number three on the depth chart behind veterans Billy Smith and Roland Melanson. Hrudey went on to play 15 seasons in the NHL—six with the Islanders, and seven with the Los Angeles Kings, including 1993 when they lost in the Stanley Cup final to Montreal. He played his final two years with the San Jose Sharks and finished with a record of 271–265–88, a 3.43 goals against average, and 17 shutouts before retiring in 1998.

He was also involved in a marathon overtime playoff game in 1987, making a playoff record 73 saves as his Islanders finally prevailed after almost 69 extra minutes, defeating Washington, 3–2.

Brett Hull

A Goal in His First Game

He is one of the most prolific scorers in NHL history, a certainty to be inducted into the Hockey Hall of Fame. There are a lot of things Brett Hull was as a hockey player and one thing he certainly was not—a can't-miss prospect.

Although Hull obviously had famous bloodlines—he is the son of the legendary Golden Jet, Bobby Hull—as a kid Brett played provincial junior hockey in Penticton, B.C., a level below major junior. A little overweight at the time, Hull clearly had skills and scoring ability, but the scouts had reservations about his ability to be a good pro.

In fact, he was twice passed over in the draft, but his scoring ability earned him a scholarship at the University of Minnesota-Duluth and he was finally drafted, albeit 117th overall, in the sixth round, by the Calgary Flames in 1984.

In 1986, he was signed and added to the Flames' roster during the playoffs, making his NHL debut in game three of the Stanley Cup finals against the Montreal Canadiens. He hit the post with his first shot using a borrowed stick. He had sent his own sticks home after the end of his college season.

Hull played twice that spring and spent the majority of the following season with the Flames' farm team in Moncton. But he did play five games with Calgary, making his regular-season debut on November 13, 1986, against the Hartford Whalers.

Of all the goal-scoring exploits that would follow, it was the first regular-season game and the first goal that created the greatest day for Hull. "Playing in my first NHL regular-season game with Calgary was my greatest day. The relief of finally reaching my goal of playing in the NHL and actually scoring the game-winning goal was more than I could ask."

Hull broke a 3–3 tie with a goal in the third period to give the Flames the win. That game and that goal gave him a sense of making it, a feeling of belonging. "Now I could say I played in the greatest hockey league in the world and no one could ever take that away from me, no matter what happened. Because I don't think there is anything as special as all the hard work and all the breaks and all you do growing up to try and become a professional hockey player. It's that moment of finally reaching that first game and saying, 'I did it,' because without the first game there is never a second one. To score in that game was great."

What happened next, of course, was pretty terrific. In an effort to add some key pieces to help them win a Stanley Cup, the Flames dealt Hull and Steve Bozek to the St. Louis Blues for defenceman Rob Ramage and goaltender Rick Wamsley on March 7, 1988, just before the trade deadline. At the time, Flames' general manager Cliff Fletcher predicted he had traded away a future 50-goal scorer, but he also believed Ramage and Wamsley could bring Calgary the Stanley Cup.

Fletcher was right on both counts. The following season the Flames beat Montreal to win the Cup, while that same season Hull began to flourish with the Blues, scoring 41 goals. The next season he scored 72 and won the Lady Byng Trophy. Then in 1990–91 he had 86, earning the Hart and Pearson Trophies. He followed that with a 70-goal season.

November 13, 1986   Civic Center, Hartford

☆ ☆ ☆ **Career Highlights** ☆ ☆ ☆

- Finished his career with 741 goals.
- Scored 50 goals in 49 games. He was just the fifth player to reach 50 goals in his team's first 50 games or less, tying for fourth fastest ever.
- Along with his father Bobby, Hull is one half of the only father-son combination to each record 1,000 career points.

Hull early in his career with Calgary.

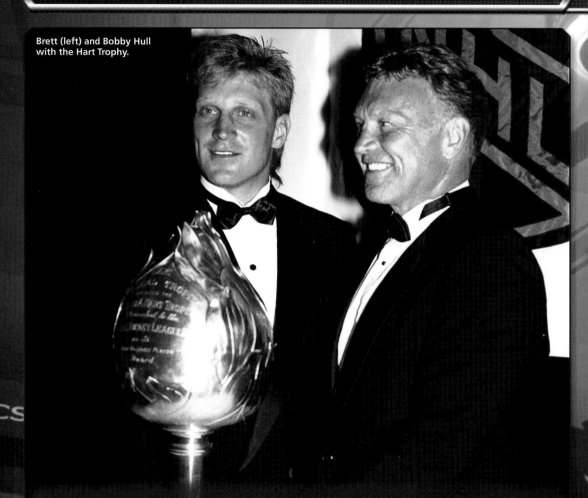

Brett (left) and Bobby Hull
with the Hart Trophy.

Although he was born in Belleville, Ontario, and spent a large part of his life
in Winnipeg and Vancouver, when it came to hockey Brett Hull decided he was
an American. Some of his siblings were born in the U.S. but he decided to play
for the Americans in large part because, early on, there wasn't much interest on
the part of Hockey Canada in having him play for Canada. Hull debuted with
the U.S. at the 1986 World Championships in Moscow. He was also a key player
when the U.S. upset Canada to win the first World Cup of Hockey in 1996, the
final game played in Montreal. Hull was prominent when the American team
won silver at the 2002 Salt Lake Games, losing, ironically, to Canada in the final.

One of his greatest memories from St. Louis was standing next to Wayne Gretzky for the national anthem after number 99 was traded to the Blues.

Hull moved on after 11 seasons in St. Louis, signing as a free agent with the Dallas Stars, where he won his first Stanley Cup in 1999, scoring a controversial Cup-winning goal in overtime of game six against Dominik Hasek and the Buffalo Sabres. There was a huge debate as to whether Hull had his foot in the crease, which was illegal at the time, when the goal was scored.

Years later in an interview, Hull remained adamant the goal was good: "It's not my fault the NHL changed the rules for control of the puck in the crease without telling anyone."

He joined the Detroit Red Wings as a free agent in the summer of 2001 and won another Cup at the end of that season. Before retiring in October 2005, the "Golden Brett" played five games with the Phoenix Coyotes, wearing his father's famous number 9, which the team had retired in honour of Phoenix's origins in Winnipeg, where Bobby Hull had a distinguished career in the WHA.

Along the way, Hull earned 1,391 points, making him and Bobby the only father and son combination in NHL history to each score 1,000 points. When he scored his 600th goal they became the only father and son duo to reach that milestone. He finished with 741 regular-season goals, becoming just the sixth player ever to reach 700, and finished third all-time in goals behind only Wayne Gretzky and Gordie Howe.

Hull scored lots of goals and had lots of great moments and memories in hockey, but none brings the feeling that he still has whenever he remembers that first night. And he thinks back to that game often, especially now that he's in management with the Stars and he sees the young players trying to do the same thing he did so many years ago.

"Seeing the kids doing the same things, going through the same things, brings back that memory. Playing that game and scoring that goal in that game is a constant memory and I get a warm feeling from it every time."

Hull with his patented off-wing one-timer.

Jarome Iginla

One Great Day

One night Jarome Iginla was sitting at home watching the highlights of the Stanley Cup playoffs on television. The next day he was in the highlights. "Literally, that's what happened."

Iginla had just finished a successful third season in the Western Hockey League with the Kamloops Blazers, losing in the division final in six games to Spokane. His phone rang and he was told he was being called up to the Calgary Flames, who were down 2–0 to the Chicago Blackhawks in their opening-round playoff series heading home to Calgary for game three.

"That was my greatest day, my first NHL game. The night before, literally, we had just lost out in junior in Kamloops, and I went home and watched the highlights. I'm a big hockey fan and I wanted to see how Calgary was doing. The next day I'm centering a line with Theo Fleury and German Titov and going into the corners with Chris Chelios. Jeremy Roenick is out there and I'm shooting on Eddie Belfour.

Jarome Iginla against the Leafs.

Iginla holds the
Frank Gehry-designed
World Cup trophy in 2004.

One Great Day

★ ★ ★ Career Highlights ★ ★ ★

- Runner-up to Bryan Berard for the Calder Trophy in 1997.
- Twice represented Canada at the Olympics, winning gold in 2002.
- A catcher on the Canadian national junior baseball team in the early 1990s.

"Iggy" does what he does best—scores.

His full name is, wait for it, Jarome Arthur-Leigh Adekunle Tij Junior Elvis Iginla. Here is how it breaks down. Arthur-Leigh was his father's middle name. Adekunle was his father's first name in Nigeria before he came to Canada as an 18-year-old. His father changed his named to Elvis because he liked it. Tij, which Jarome named his son, was short for Tijani, the name of his father's father in Nigeria. Iginla means "big tree."

"All within one day and totally unexpected. But what a way to start. It's a playoff game, a packed house in Calgary, and with all the emotions and excitement."

But there was an added significance.

"That day, I had made the NHL. Within that one day, you always hope it is going to happen, you're confident it is going to happen, but you never know if you are going to make it, no matter how close you are, until you get there. And I was there. That was the day I'd always wanted since I started playing at age seven.

"That day, if I never played again, and thankfully obviously I have, I had made the NHL and I remember thinking I hadn't just made it, but to be a part of playoff game, too, was special.

"There wasn't a lot of time for build up, or to get nervous, but it was probably one of the most exciting days I've had. I remember going into the corner with Chelios. I think I knocked him down; I was pretty excited about that."

Iginla had an assist in that first game and a goal in the second and was plus-two in those two playoff games, which the Flames lost 7–5 and then 2–1 in triple overtime. Little did he know that these were the last playoff games the Flames would play for eight years until Iginla led them to within one win of the Stanley Cup in 2004.

Iginla, who grew up outside Edmonton, was actually drafted by the Dallas Stars 11th overall in 1995, after he had won back-to-back Memorial Cup titles with Kamloops. That year the draft was held in Edmonton, which was also special to the Albertan.

In his final year of junior he won gold with Team Canada at the 1996 World Junior Championship. He scored 63 goals and 136 points with the Blazers and was named WHL player of the year. Part way through that season the Stars traded him to Calgary with Corey Millen in exchange for veteran Joe Nieuwendyk.

In 2002, Iginla reached new heights of success. He won the Art Ross Trophy, leading the NHL with 96 points, as well as the Rocket Richard Trophy for his league-leading 52 goals. He also won the Lester B. Pearson Award as most valuable player as selected by NHL players. More significant, he won Olympic gold with Team Canada in Salt Lake City, scoring twice in the final game.

In 2004, he tied for the league lead with 41 goals and led the Flames to a seven-game loss to the Tampa Bay Lightning in the Stanley Cup finals. That fall he helped Canada win the World Cup of Hockey. He was a finalist for the Hart Trophy in 2008, when he had 50 goals and a career-high 98 points.

"I think of draft day being at home, and that was amazing. I think of winning the gold medal with Canada. Those moments would be right up there for sure, but I think actually playing my first NHL game, getting called up in the playoffs, was so surreal. That is what I dreamed about, getting to the NHL and winning the Stanley Cup, and the first part of it came true that day.

"My family got to watch. It felt like a shared moment because for a long time, while it had been a dream of mine, it had partly been their dream, too, in helping me reach mine. Playing in that game, being on the ice with NHLers was amazing. You play that one and they can't take it away. It meant I had made it."

A Kid Watches the Rocket Explode

Most kids dream of one day playing in the NHL, and Dick Irvin was no different. As for so many, though, that dream never did come true, although Irvin made it to the NHL in a different way.

"I was 12 years old and my father [Dick Irvin, Sr.] was coaching the Montreal Canadiens. My dad used to commute to Montreal. We kept our home in Regina and when the season started, he'd move into a hotel in Montreal, The Mount Royal. He stayed there for 11 years.

"At Christmas time, my mom and sister and I would fly to Montreal and stay with him. It was the 1944 Christmas that was really special. The previous year the Canadiens had won the Stanley Cup. They had put together the Punch Line of Elmer Lach, Toe Blake, and Rocket Richard. In the 1944–45 season, Rocket really became the Rocket. It's when he became the number one name in hockey.

"Back then, because of the war, teams only had 14 players in uniform so there was lots of room on the bench. When I visited my dad, he would put me on the end of the bench.

Dick Irvin, Jr.

Hockey and broadcasting always seemed to go hand-in-hand for the Irvin family, even if they didn't know at the time how long it was going to last. While Dick Irvin, Jr., was educated at McGill University, he always loved broadcasting and, obviously, became one of the top hockey broadcasters ever in Canada, as a colour commentator, interviewer, and play-by-play man. His father, the legendary player and coach, actually played in the first professional game broadcast on radio, a game between the Regina Capitals and the Edmonton Eskimos on March 15, 1923, on CKCK Regina. Dick, Sr., later coached in the first televised game, which was between the Canadiens and Chicago in Montreal in October 1952 on a CBC affiliate.

James Dickinson "Dick" Irvin, Sr., and his son, Dick, Jr.

☆ ☆ ☆ Career Highlights ☆ ☆ ☆

- Honoured by the Hockey Hall of Fame in the broadcasters' category in 1988.
- Author of several best-selling books including *Now Back To You Dick*, *The Habs*, and *Behind The Bench*.
- Covered more than 2,000 games on television and radio.

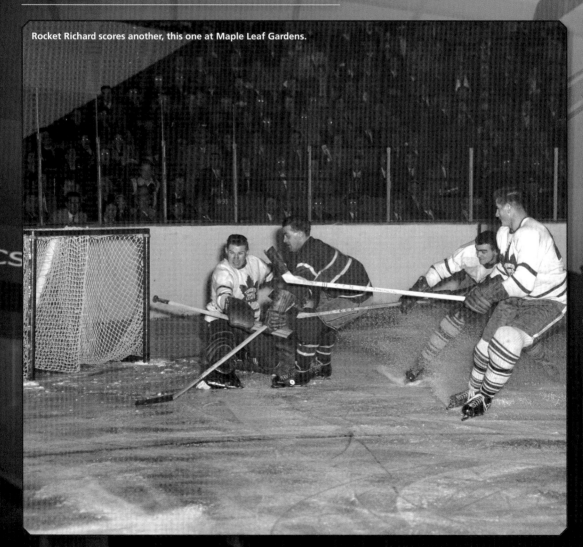

Rocket Richard scores another, this one at Maple Leaf Gardens.

"December 28, 1944, that was my greatest day. The Canadiens were playing the Detroit Red Wings, a game that was famous for many reasons. That was the day Rocket had moved from one apartment to another. He spent the whole day moving. There were no morning skates back then, so he got up and did it himself with a friend. When he got to the rink that night, he said to my dad he didn't think he could play. He was tired and a little sore from carrying the furniture. It was a full day's move.

"My dad said to him, 'Put on your uniform; you might get a couple of goals.' Well, that night he got five goals and three assists. He set the all-time points record. The previous record was seven, held by Syd Howe. I can remember it like it was yesterday. I was sitting at the end of the bench and after one of the goals, the Rocket came down and sat right beside me. The trainer came over and put a towel around his neck and I'm thinking the whole building is looking at me saying, 'Who is the kid sitting on the Montreal Canadiens' bench next to Rocket?'

"It turned out to be a 9–1 final. On the last goal—I think it was Blake who scored it—my dad was yelling at the referee as he skated by the bench, saying the Rocket got a point, he got an assist, because he knew it would set the record with eight points. Well, number 9 got the assist whether he deserved it or not. He got it, the eighth point, and set the record.

"Harry Lumley was the goaltender for Detroit that night. I think it was his second or third game in the NHL. He was just 18, but guys like that were playing because of the war, so that night the Red Wings had a teenage goaltender. Ten years later, Bert Olmstead tied the record with eight points in a game and that stood until 1976 when Darryl Sittler had his 10-point night with the Maple Leafs.

"The Rocket always mentioned that game as being a highlight of his career, or the game he remembered the most. He was a guy, like Guy Lafleur, who never remembered goals he scored. He was such an instinctive player, they just happened. Guy played on instinct and Rocket was the same.

"That Christmas trip, I sat on the bench four times. I went on a trip to Boston, Toronto, and New York, then that game in Montreal."

Irvin, of course, also made it to the NHL in another way. Although he studied at McGill University in Montreal, he loved broadcasting and wound up covering Canadiens' games for more than 30 years on local radio and television and with CBC's *Hockey Night in Canada*, where for many years he worked alongside the legendary Danny Gallivan, serving as one of the first colour commentators.

He also became an accomplished hockey author and was inducted into the Hockey Hall of Fame in 1988, and in 2004 was inducted into the Canadian Association of Broadcasters Hall of Fame.

In the end, he never made it to the NHL as a player or coach, like his famous father, but he did have a profound attachment to and influence on the game as a broadcaster, author, and historian.

And he was on the Canadiens' bench on December 28, 1944—his greatest day in hockey and the night of one of Rocket Richard's greatest performances.

Winning Gold with the Juniors

It's ironic, but Jeff Jackson remembers alternately wondering and deep down fearing that one truly great moment in his hockey career might wind up being *the* greatest moment when it was over.

And it was.

"My greatest moment was a really great moment, there's no doubt about that. It was in the 1985 World Junior Championship in Helsinki. We won the gold medal, the first Canadian junior team to win the gold in Europe. Back then it was a round-robin format, so you'd play every team once. I remember beating the Russians, 5–0, in our third last game."

That game was memorable for a thundering hit Wendel Clark administered on Soviet defenceman Mikhail Tatarinov, sending him out of the tournament.

"Wendel really laid him out. It was one of Wendel's prototypical hits where he lifted the guy's feet off the ice before slamming into the boards. It changed the whole game. That win made us 5–0 in the tournament. We tied Finland, 4–4, in our next game on New Year's Eve. We gave up a two-goal lead in that one.

"Then we played the Czechs in the final game. We tied them 2–2. Wendel scored with about six minutes to go [6:17 to be precise]. He had been playing defence, but played up front in the third period. We knew all we had to do was tie it to win, so we held on for gold. Dominik Hasek was their goalie. It was pretty cool.

"I played on a line with Brian Bradley and Adam Creighton. We were the top three scorers on the team and I got lots of ice time. It was great. I remember after that Czech game standing there for the national anthem, doing that whole singing thing, which back in 1985 was kind of new. The '82 team had won and we were the next ones and I think we were the first to sing the Canadian anthem afterwards.

"Just playing for your country, winning gold and doing it in Europe was special. Back then it was pretty much just the team there—the coaches and a few officials—because it was in Europe. There weren't any big entourages. It was just the team there enjoying the moment. It was pretty good. I remember standing there on the blue line—I was only 19—thinking I hope this isn't my greatest moment in hockey, but it might be."

Indeed, it was. Jackson, who played parts of eight seasons with four different NHL teams, was drafted 28th overall by the Toronto Maple Leafs in 1983. After the junior tournament and his junior season ended in Hamilton, he played 17 games with the Leafs to close out the season.

It was at the start of the previous season, though, that he had another great moment. It happened on Thursday, September 15, 1983.

"It was my first NHL game at Maple Leaf Gardens and I lined up to start the game at left wing. On right wing for the opposing team—it was the Washington Capitals—was Ken Houston, who was my childhood idol from Dresden, Ontario, my hometown.

Team Canada celebrates its gold medal at the 1985 World Junior Championship

Even after he retired from hockey, Jeff Jackson never really left the game. He merely traded in his stick for a briefcase. Jackson, who was named the director of hockey administration for the Toronto Maple Leafs on June 23, 2006, practiced law in Toronto after he retired. He served as a legal counsel, acting for companies, performers, and athletes. He also represented a number of NHL teams preparing their salary arbitration cases. With the Leafs, Jackson handles collective bargaining related assignments, contract negotiations, salary arbitration, and salary cap management.

⭐ ⭐ ⭐
Career Highlights
⭐ ⭐ ⭐

- Selected 28th overall by the Toronto Maple Leafs in the 1983 Entry Draft.
- Had his best statistical year with Quebec in 1987–88, finishing with 27 points and a plus-5 rating.
- Earned his law degree after retiring.

Jackson with the Brantford Alexanders (above) and with the Nordiques (right).

"He's several [12] years older than me, but I always looked up to him. He taught me in hockey school and for me to have my first shift in the NHL lined up against him was special. He tapped me on the pads at the start of the game and said, 'Go get 'em, kid.'

"It was pretty cool and it was very unusual that I would have that chance. We actually beat them 6–2 that night. Russ Courtnall, Dan Hodgson, and I played on a line and we got a couple of goals. And then we all got sent back to junior the next day. It was an exhibition game, but it was our first actual game at Maple Leaf Gardens.

"Growing up, Bryan Trottier was my favourite player and I loved the New York Islanders, but Ken was the hometown guy who I really looked up to. When he came home in the summer, he'd always come over to our house and play grass hockey with me. I was just a little kid and to play the first shift against him was a unique experience. He and I still laugh about it when I see him now.

Jeff Jackson

"Think about it, that many years apart, from a small town, right wing versus left wing, to be matched up against him. And then he taps me on the pad. I came around behind the net on my first shift at full speed and I had my head down. He really could have rammed me, but as he went by me and missed me he said, 'Keep your head up, kid.'" That day also happened to be Houston's 30th birthday.

Jackson also played with the New York Rangers, Quebec Nordiques, and one game with the Chicago Blackhawks before retiring in 1992. Now a lawyer, he is an assistant general manager with the Maple Leafs.

Mike Keenan

Bringing the Cup to Broadway

The sign, held by a fan in the seats at Madison Square Garden that night, said it all: NOW I CAN DIE IN PEACE.

"It's funny, though, I had been in situations like that before when there was a huge sense of relief when it was over, but not this time," said Mike Keenan. "It was all about celebrating."

The party, after all, had been on hold for more than 54 years. But a New York Rangers' team that had been loaded with veterans, many of whom had achieved great success in Edmonton, and an experienced coach finally managed to chase away the demons or the curse or whatever it was that had prevented the Stanley Cup from going to New York City for more than half a century.

That night, those derisive chants of "1940" the Rangers used to hear all the time were replaced by the chants of "1994." But it wasn't easy, just as you would expect.

That season, the Rangers had finished first overall with 52 victories. They cruised through the first round of the playoffs, sweeping the arch-rival New York Islanders, who were seeded eighth. In the second round the Blueshirts breezed by the seventh-seeded Washington Capitals in five games. But then it got interesting in the Conference finals against the third-seeded New Jersey Devils.

The Rangers lost the series opener at home in double overtime but won the next two games before the Devils shut down the New York offence and beat them 3–1 and 4–1. The series headed back to the Meadowlands for what seemed like another inevitable Rangers' conclusion, but the day before that sixth game, Rangers' captain Mark Messier stepped up and guaranteed a win.

"Mark was sending a message to his teammates that he believed together we could win. He put on an amazing performance to make sure it happened."

In that sixth game, Messier scored three times to lead the Rangers to a 4–2 win and set up a seventh game back at Madison Square Garden, which the Rangers won, 2–1, when Stephane Matteau scored in double overtime to send them to the finals for the first time since 1979.

Up against the Vancouver Canucks, the Cinderella team from the west, the Rangers again lost the series opener at home in overtime. Brian Leetch hit the crossbar at one end, and the Canucks went down to score the winner at the other.

But their experience and poise helped the Rangers to bounce back and they won the next three games, allowing the Canucks just four goals. That set the stage for a game-five Stanley Cup celebration at home, the first time the team had ever been in a position to win a Cup at the Garden. The celebration plans, however, got ahead of the work at hand.

That night, the Canucks were leading 3–0 by the third minute of the second period. Even though the Rangers scrambled to pull even by the midway point, Vancouver took the lead 29 seconds later and cruised to a 6–3 win. New York's parade hopes were given another jolt two nights later when the Canucks put together a 4–1 win, forcing coach Keenan to prepare for a game seven.

"Even though we were up 3–1 in the series and had to play a seventh game, the team was very confident and very poised. We had a lot of experience and a lot of leadership in our room."

Mike Keenan

Success came quickly in the NHL for Mike Keenan. In his first season with Philadelphia, 1984–85, Keenan went to the Stanley Cup final. Two years later, he did the same, both times losing to the Edmonton Oilers. In that summer of 1987, Keenan teamed up with a lot of those Oilers, the likes of Wayne Gretzky and Mark Messier, to lead Team Canada to victory in the Canada Cup, which turned out to be one of the greatest international hockey series ever.

Canada lost the first game of the best-of-three final to the Soviets in Montreal, 6–5 in overtime, after battling back from a 4–1 deficit. In game two in Hamilton, Canada led 3–1 and 5–3 but required a goal from Mario Lemieux, set up by Gretzky, in double overtime to win 6–5. In the third game, Canada was shocked early as the Soviets took a 3–0 lead eight minutes into the game. But the Canadians again battled back and led 5–4 after two periods. The Soviets tied it, but with 1:26 remaining Lemieux scored the historic winning goal, again set up by Gretzky, to give Canada another 6–5 victory. The final scores matched the final score in game eight of the historic 1972 Canada-Soviet Union Summit Series.

"The 1987 Canada Cup was an exceptional challenge for a very young coach," Keenan said. "It was the last time we beat the Soviet Union as a communist country. They were two superstar teams. When we won, there was a sense of relief. I was much younger then, and that series took on a bigger life than the others. It wasn't just hockey, it was capitalism vs. communism, country vs. country, and losing just wasn't going to be accepted. I remember in the last game we were down 3–0 early in the first period and I said to myself, 'Well, you better do something or get the car and start driving north and never be heard from again.'" Keenan decided to give his grinders more work and they got Canada back in the game, setting the stage for the stars to close the deal. "It was '72 for another generation and these teams might have been better and better prepared. The players were at an optimum level, in the prime of their careers. Gretzky and Messier were 26, winning Cups and playing their best. Gretz says that was the best hockey he had ever played."

★ ★ ★ **Career Highlights** ★ ★ ★

- Only Scotty Bowman and Al Arbour reached 600 coaching victories at a younger age than Keenan.

- Won the Jack Adams award as coach of the year in 1985 with Philadelphia.

- Won the Stanley Cup (1994), two Canada Cups (1987 and 1991), one Calder Cup (1983), and a Canadian national university title (1984).

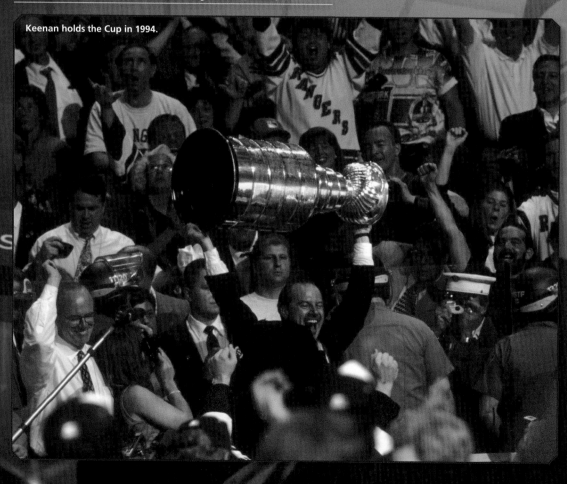

Keenan holds the Cup in 1994.

When it was over, Messier mentioned how Keenan had provided a lot of that leadership and had given, on the eve of game seven, one of the greatest speeches he had heard in hockey.

"I told the players they should be proud of themselves no matter what happened in that game. I told them to play hard and enjoy the moment. This is what we all dreamed about, playing a seventh game on home ice to win the Stanley Cup."

The seventh game was a classic. The Rangers took a 2–0 first-period lead, but the Canucks scored shorthanded to cut the lead. Messier scored later on a power play to put the Rangers up 3–1. The Canucks scored a power-play goal themselves early in the third, but the Rangers managed to hang on, 3–2, as the Garden erupted in tears and cheers.

"I remember when we finally won it, I was standing on the bench and all the players were celebrating on the ice. People were in the stands crying. I was just standing on the bench taking it all in. And the players were passing around the Stanley Cup at centre and all of a sudden Mark has it and he brings it over to the bench and hands me the Stanley Cup.

"It was an incredible feeling. He kind of surprised me by doing it. I can't remember ever seeing that happen before. So now he hands me the Stanley Cup and I remember thinking, well, that only took 10 years to happen. But that moment was the culmination of 10 years as an NHL coach and years before that.

"It is the greatest day for me because winning the Stanley Cup is why you are involved. And then the circumstances surrounding it, that city, that franchise, the 54-year wait. I have been fortunate to win at various levels, in university, the Calder Cup in the AHL. I was able to get to the finals and win two Canada Cups in 1987 and 1991. But that was the greatest.

"When it was over, it was more celebration than relief. I had felt relief in situations before, but not this time. It was a unique opportunity and the reward for lots and lots of hard work. To get the final result you want on the biggest stage in the world was truly amazing."

For Keenan, the wait to win had been excruciating at times. He had been in the league a decade and it was his ninth season behind the bench. As a rookie NHL coach in 1985, he took the Philadelphia Flyers to the finals where they were beaten in five games by the Edmonton Oilers. Two years later, the Oilers beat his Flyers in seven games. In 1992, he took the Chicago Blackhawks, another long-suffering franchise, to the finals where they were swept by Mario Lemieux and a great Pittsburgh team.

"It was my fourth attempt in the finals and for that reason it was special. I'm not sure winning it validates you as a coach because to win you need a good team and good players who stay healthy, but you want to be known as a guy who wins big games."

As the sign said, Rangers' fans could now die in peace.

One Game Closer to Victory

In the eyes of many he was one of the greatest—if not *the* greatest—Toronto Maple Leafs' players ever. He helped lead them to four Stanley Cup victories, including three straight from 1962–64, and the last one the franchise has ever won, in 1967. In that year, Dave Keon won the Conn Smythe Trophy as the most valuable player in the playoffs.

He won the Calder Trophy, as top rookie, scoring 20 goals in 1960–61. He twice won the Lady Byng, as most gentlemanly player, with a mere two minutes in penalties all season in each of those years.

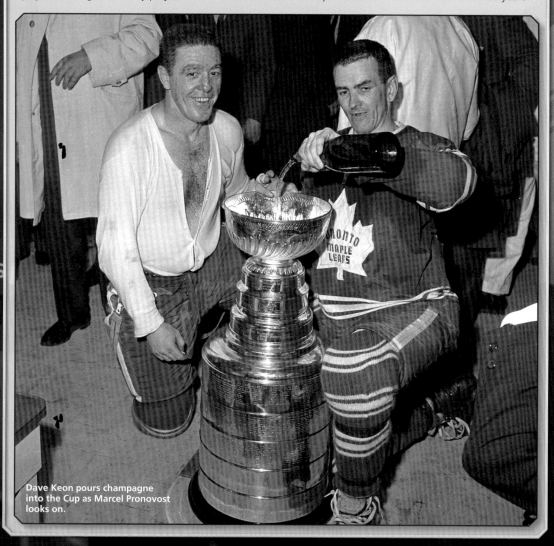

Dave Keon pours champagne into the Cup as Marcel Pronovost looks on.

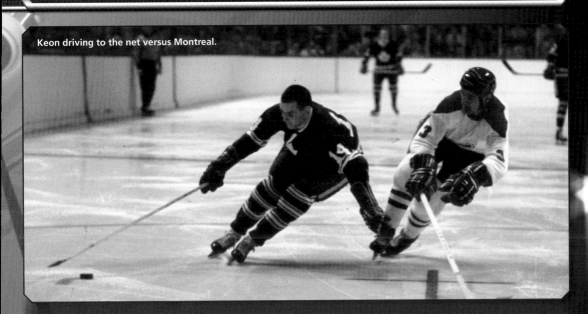

Keon driving to the net versus Montreal.

It may not have been the greatest day in hockey for Dave Keon, but for many of his fans it was. The date was February 17, 2007, at the Air Canada Centre in Toronto. After years of refusing to take part in any team-related activities with the Leafs, Keon finally agreed to appear in Toronto in a pre-game ceremony to honour the 1967 Stanley Cup champion team. Keon had long been at odds with the organization, dating back to a messy departure from the team under owner Harold Ballard in 1975. His unhappiness continued because he was upset with how retired Leafs' players were treated and how sweater numbers were "honoured," not retired outright. But this time he finally agreed to appear because of the team. "John [general manager Ferguson] called and said they wanted to pay tribute to the '67 team and asked if I would take part. It was a tribute to our team and I wanted to be a part of it." Keon had previously agreed to attend the closing of Maple Leaf Gardens, but like some others refused to attend when the invitations turned out to be form letters and the players believed they had to attend at their own expense. For the night honouring the 1967 team at the Air Canada Centre, the Leafs paid to fly the out-of-town players to Toronto and provided accommodation as well. The invitations were also personalized, followed by a call from Ferguson. When Keon stepped onto the ice that night, he was greeted by a one-minute standing ovation. For one night, at least, there was another greatest moment in Toronto.

★ ★ ★

Career Highlights

★ ★ ★

- **Won the Conn Smythe Trophy in the 1967 playoffs.**
- **Had 986 points in 1,296 NHL games.**
- **In his 15 years as a Maple Leaf, he scored 20 goals or more 11 times.**

Keon becomes Leafs' captain.

He was a graceful skater who was known for his defensive excellence, checking acumen, and penalty-killing brilliance. But he was just as good with the puck, scoring goals and setting them up. He scored a record eight short-handed goals one season.

There is no shortage of good memories from his 15 seasons in Toronto, the first eight at a time when the Leafs were good and successful. But much like his time in Toronto, Dave Keon's greatest day was bittersweet.

"There were a lot of good moments, but I would have to say my greatest day was March 20, 1963. I scored a goal with 10 seconds left in the third period against the Montreal Canadiens to clinch first place overall. That's the last time Toronto ever finished first overall and won the Prince of Wales Trophy."

That was back in the old six-team league, of course. With Keon's goal the Leafs managed a comeback 3–3 tie, mathematically eliminating the Canadiens for the hunt for first place. Toronto finished on top with 82 points in 70 games, followed by Chicago with 81 and Montreal with 79.

"We had two games left on the weekend with Detroit, but that night clinched it. I remember we pulled our goalie, who was Johnny Bower that night, and we either had to tie or beat Montreal to take first. We were up in the game, then the Canadiens went ahead. But with 10 seconds left Nevy [Bob Nevin] got the puck and passed to me and I beat Jacques Plante.

"Finishing first was kind of a big thing. It's something we really wanted to do, especially against the Canadiens. We were always fighting the Canadiens and we'd always wind up one-two in wins, but we'd usually fall short.

"Winning the Cup was always big, of course, but that year we were able to finish first, then went on to win the Cup. I scored some big goals in the finals. That year, in '63, I scored two shorthanded goals in game five of the final."

That was in a 3–1 Toronto victory that eliminated the Red Wings in five games. It was a playoff record for shorthanded goals in a game.

But while winning the Cup and setting the record was exciting, this was a bittersweet time for Keon personally. His greatest day in hockey, March 20, 1963, quickly gave way to the worst day in his life a day later, and then into his most confused day right after that.

"I went the full range of emotions, from one end of the spectrum to the other in a day. My best day was the 20th, when we clinched first. My worst day was the 21st, when my son died. He was 18 months old. He was sick from the time he was born. He spent 16 of those 18 months in hospital, so it wasn't a shock, but when it happens it is still crushing and confusing. And then the 22nd was my 23rd birthday. In three days I had gone from the top of the world to the bottom to I don't know what is going on."

Keon's career with the Leafs ended awkwardly, with owner Harold Ballard publicly criticizing his captain, in large part because Ballard didn't want to pay the veteran star. Keon eventually signed with the World Hockey Association and quietly retired in 1982.

He was inducted into the Hockey Hall of Fame in 1986 after a distinguished 22-year career, but for the longest time remained estranged from the franchise he had helped make great.

Pat LaFontaine

A Hat Trick in Career Game Two

Every kid with a dream has those special moments growing up that they never forget and that often ultimately influence their lives. Pat LaFontaine was no different.

"It was back in February 1980, and the United States Olympic team had essentially just won the gold medal at Lake Placid. It was on my 15th birthday, February 22nd, when Mike Eruzione scored the goal."

The goal was not just any goal; it was the game winner in Team USA's second-to-last game of the Olympic tournament, which gave the Americans a shocking 4-3 victory over the mighty Soviet Union, one of the biggest upsets ever. You may remember it better as the Miracle on Ice.

Young Pat LaFontaine.

"That same year, in the spring, my father had my brother and me home for spring cleaning. We were out in the yard working and he yelled at us to come inside. The New York Islanders were in overtime against the Philadelphia Flyers. Picture it. It's national television. I'm 15 years old. I run inside and we're watching as Lorne Henning takes a pass, then he passes to John Tonelli, he passes to Bobby Nystrom, and Nystrom tips it in and the Islanders win their first Stanley Cup. I remember my brother and I were jumping up and down, excited, thinking what a feeling it must have been for the Islanders."

Fast forward four years.

"You have to remember, I was raised in Michigan. There were a few guys—Reed Larson, Kenny Morrow, Mark Wells—who made it to the NHL, but there weren't a lot of NHL players from Michigan. I had aspirations to get a college scholarship one day. That's what I was hoping for. Little in my wildest dreams did I ever think that I could play for an Olympic team, fulfill that dream, and a week later join the New York Islanders, who had won four Stanley Cups, and fulfill another dream."

But that is exactly what happened to LaFontaine, who left home at age 16 in 1982 to play junior hockey in Verdun, Quebec, for a season to chase the dream. He won the scoring championship that year with a remarkable 104 goals, 20 more than Mario Lemieux, and 130 assists. He was named the top junior player in Canada and led Verdun to the

Pat LaFontaine, the night of his greatest day, March 3, 1984, at Maple Leaf Gardens

On April 18, 1987, while playing for the New York Islanders, Pat LaFontaine was involved in the ninth longest overtime in Stanley Cup playoff history. The Islanders had trailed the Washington Capitals 3–1 in the series, but had battled back to force a seventh game that wouldn't end, at least not until LaFontaine performed his magic in the fourth overtime. It was the first time in 36 years a game had gone that long. That night, at 8:42 of the fourth overtime period, a total 68 minutes and 42 seconds of extra time, LaFontaine's screen shot from the point eluded Capitals' goaltender Bob Mason to give the Islanders a 3–2 win. "I will never forget that game, to battle back the way we did, to battle through that game, was amazing," said LaFontaine. "It was really something special and helped my career."

⭐ ⭐ ⭐
Career Highlights
⭐ ⭐ ⭐

- **Played 15 NHL seasons and finished with 1,013 points.**
- **In his one season with Verdun in junior he scored 104 goals and had 234 points.**
- **Won the Masterton Memorial Trophy in 1995.**

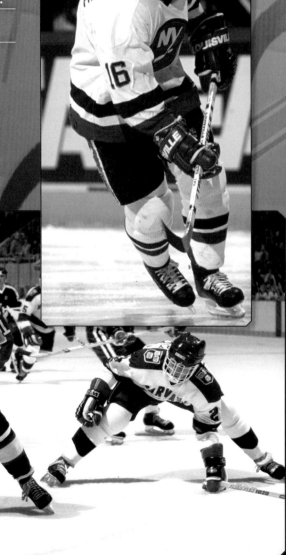

Pat LaFontaine

LaFontaine with Team USA.

Memorial Cup finals, where the team lost to Portland.

That summer, he was drafted third overall by the Islanders. Had the Islanders not selected him, Detroit would have taken the Michigan native with the fourth pick. Instead, the Red Wings wound up with Steve Yzerman. The following season, LaFontaine decided to play for the U.S. national team and ultimately the Olympic team in the 1984 Sarajevo Games, following on the heels of Eruzione and the Miracle on Ice team.

When the Olympics were over, LaFontaine, 19, joined the Islanders for the final 15 games of the regular season and 16 more games in the playoffs, but his most memorable day was his second NHL game ever, on March 3, 1984.

LaFontaine hoists the World Cup in 1996.

"It was my greatest day in hockey. That night, I'm sitting there before the game, wearing an Islanders jersey and I kept thinking about when I was 15, my dad and my brother and myself, watching that overtime goal. My second NHL game. It was at Maple Leaf Gardens, against Toronto, on March 3.

"My right winger is Bobby Nystrom and my left winger is John Tonelli. I'm pinching myself thinking, is this real? They played the national anthem, my dad's there at the game, and I'm looking back at my childhood and thinking of all the sacrifices my parents made and how this all happened so fast.

"Believe it or not, we won that game 11-6. I got my first NHL goal, my first NHL hat trick [against goaltenders Allan Bester and Rick St. Croix], my first assist, my first penalty. And Bobby Nystrom, John Tonelli, and I were the three stars of the game. That was a pretty special night. I was fortunate to have a lot of special nights in my career, but that was my greatest day."

And that particular day on the calendar, March 3, would be significant for LaFontaine later in life.

"Twenty-two years later, Donny Meehan, a dear friend and my agent calls and says that Larry Quinn [president of Buffalo] and the Sabres want to retire my jersey, here are a few dates to pick from. Obviously, it's a tremendous honour. Not thinking about it, I said March 3 against Toronto sounds great. It wasn't until a month or two later, I'm in my house, and I look up on the wall at the first goal, the puck, and it said March 3, 1984. So 22 years later, against the same team, the Toronto Maple Leafs, the Buffalo Sabres retire my sweater. Twenty-two years to the day! Who would have thought?"

LaFontaine had a terrific NHL career, playing 16 seasons with the Islanders, Buffalo, and New York Rangers before concussion-related problems forced him to retire. He finished with 468 goals and 545 assists and was inducted into the Hockey Hall of Fame in 2003.

"There are no such things as coincidences. There are no coincidences in life. Things happen for a reason. To see things come full circle like that, on March 3, was nice closure, to say the least. It was a good sign."

There has long been this notion, and no one is really certain how it started, that European players don't want to win the Stanley Cup as much as North American players, especially Canadians. As the notion goes, Olympic gold is more important than Stanley Cup silverware to players from overseas. Not true.

At least it's not true as it applies to Detroit Red Wings' captain Nicklas Lidstrom. Lidstrom has won internationally with the Swedish national team, including gold in the 2006 Olympics in Turin, Italy. It was a great accomplishment, a proud and satisfying moment, a great day. But it wasn't his greatest day in hockey.

"Any time you have a chance to win the Stanley Cup, it is a great moment, but this latest time was great because I had a chance to wear the "C" and touch the Cup first of all the players, and being the first European captain to win made this last one really special."

When the Red Wings defeated the Pittsburgh Penguins, 3–2, in game six of the Stanley Cup finals, Lidstrom was first in line when NHL commissioner Gary Bettman presented the Stanley Cup. As such, Lidstrom became the first European-born-and-trained captain to accept the trophy.

"I've been over here for a long time and I watched Steve Yzerman hoist it three times in the past. I'm very proud of being the first European. I'm very proud of being a captain of the Red Wings. There's so much history with this team and a great tradition."

The win was the Red Wings' fourth Cup victory in 11 years. Lidstrom has been around for all four, beginning in 1997 when they swept Philadelphia in four games. But that victory was quickly tempered by a horrible limousine accident a few days later, after a team party, that left defenceman Vladimir Konstantinov crippled.

Then there was the sweep of the Washington Capitals a year later, followed by a five-game victory over Carolina in 2002 with the best team money could buy. Lidstrom won the Conn Smythe Trophy that spring as most valuable player.

Coming out of the lockout, without the ability to spend freely, the Red Wings weren't supposed to be great or dominant any more. But they have been great and Lidstrom has been among the greatest of them all, though there were playoff pains and disappointments before he finally got to hoist the Cup again.

Lidstrom became captain of the Red Wings at the start of the 2006–07 season at age 36, taking over from Yzerman, who had been captain for 20 seasons. In many ways the 2007 Cup win felt like a first for the Red Wings. It was the first for Mike Babcock as coach after Scotty Bowman. It was the first for general manager Ken Holland in the salary cap era, the first without Yzerman, and the first with a European captain.

When it came time to pass the Cup to a teammate, Lidstrom had it all figured out, too. The first to get it was veteran Dallas Drake, who had waited 14 seasons to win. Then it was winger Daniel Cleary, who had been without a team a few seasons earlier but who worked hard

Swedish captain Nicklas
Lidstrom with the Cup in 2008.

Stanley's First European Captain

☆ ☆ ☆ **Career Highlights** ☆ ☆ ☆

- **Has 938 career points, including 726 assists, in 1,252 NHL games.**
- **In his rookie season, he had 11 goals and 49 assists and was second to Pavel Bure in Calder Trophy voting.**
- **Scored the opening goal in an eventual 2–1 win over Philadelphia in game four of the 1997 finals, helping to lead the Red Wings to their first Stanley Cup in 42 years.**

Lidstrom (right) playing for Team Sweden.

Red Wings' captain Nicklas Lidstrom has had the pleasure of winning the Stanley Cup four times and in 2008 was the first European captain of a Cup winner. But it almost didn't happen. At least part of it. Back in 1998, after the Red Wings had won their first two Cups, Lidstrom gave serious thought to returning to Sweden to play, in large part because he wanted his kids to grow up and be educated in the Swedish school system. But he signed another deal with the Red Wings worth $7 million annually and has subsequently signed additional contracts. In the meantime, he has won two Stanley Cups, a Conn Smythe Trophy, and six Norris Trophies. It was well worth his while staying, though when his career is done Lidstrom will head home.

to restore his career. Cleary became the first Newfoundlander to win the trophy.

As well as the Cup victory, Lidstrom won the Norris Trophy as best defenceman in the NHL for the sixth time in seven seasons, putting him in the company of the great Bobby Orr, who won it eight straight times, and Doug Harvey, who won it seven times.

"I don't feel like I belong with those players. They played in a different era. I don't look at myself as being in the range of those players."

Perhaps not, but others do. Lidstrom's low-key nature off ice closely resembles his personality on it. He is not about style, but substance. He is consistently good, making smart plays at both ends of the rink. He doesn't play a physical style but positions himself well to win battles and control the puck.

"I think just with his everyday professionalism and the modeling he does for the rest of us and how he carries himself,

Lidstrom with the Cup in the days when Steve Yzerman was Detroit captain.

how he handles himself, how well he plays, how hard he practices, is an example to everybody," Babcock said of his captain during the finals. "And I think that's the key to leadership. Leadership is you can say some things sometime, but it's more about what you do. And to me, that's what he does for us.

"Obviously he's a gifted, gifted athlete who reads the game as well as anybody and plays in all situations. And when your best defensive defenceman is your best offensive defenceman, I think it helps because you get the puck going."

Lidstrom led all NHL defencemen in scoring during the 2007–08 regular season with 70 points (including 60 assists) in 76 games and a plus-40 rating. The six games he missed with a knee injury were the most he had missed in any one of his 16 NHL seasons. Since he began his NHL career in 1991–92, Lidstrom has the highest plus-minus of any NHLer at plus-378.

He has also appeared in 16 consecutive playoffs, a franchise record and one more than Yzerman. His 214 career playoff games also surpassed the previous mark of 196 held by Yzerman and are the most of any European player.

"It felt great being the first guy to touch the Cup on our team. Otherwise it felt the same as winning the previous ones, where you're so happy with the end result. You start training camp with a goal and that is to win the Stanley Cup."

Kevin Lowe has been involved in a lot of firsts for the Edmonton Oilers. He was the club's first NHL draft pick, selected 21st overall in 1979. He scored the first goal in franchise history in their first game, a power-play effort against the Chicago Blackhawks and Tony Esposito at 9:49 of the first period. A kid named Wayne Gretzky earned his first NHL point on that goal.

There would be many more goals and points, of course, particularly by Gretzky, and there would be considerable success, including five Stanley Cup victories in seven years with the Oilers, all but one with Gretzky on the team. And there would be another Stanley Cup victory for Lowe in 1994 with the New York Rangers when that team ended its 54-year drought.

Not surprisingly, Rangers' general manager Neil Smith purposely brought a handful of Oilers into the fold—Lowe, Mark Messier, Glenn Anderson—because they knew how to win.

"Considering I won six Stanley Cups and enjoyed success in international play, too, you might think it would be a hard question to answer, but by far my greatest day in hockey was the night the Edmonton Oilers won the Stanley Cup for the first time. It was May 19, 1984, game five against the New York Islanders. Long Island was shooting for its fifth straight Cup win and second straight over us. We learned a tough lesson the year before at the hands of those guys."

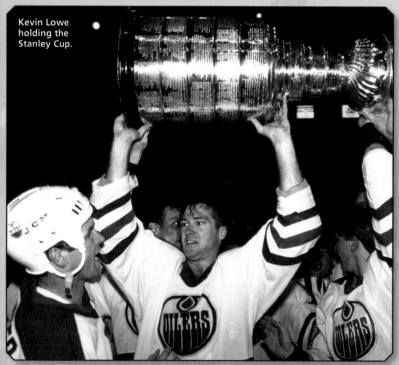

Kevin Lowe holding the Stanley Cup.

The upstart Oilers—with all that talent and firepower and all those young legs—were favoured by many to win in the spring of 1983, but the veteran Islanders taught them a thing or two about what it takes to win a championship. Using guts and guile and determination, the Islanders dug deep to produce that fourth Cup win and cement their dynasty status by sweeping the Oilers in the four-game final.

A lot of youngsters today might know him only as the general manager of the Edmonton Oilers. Chances are, many never saw him as a star defenceman and five-time Stanley Cup winner with that same team, as well as a star performer—and Cup winner— with the New York Rangers. But playing in the shadow of Wayne Gretzky and Mark Messier—and Grant Fuhr, Jari Kurri, and Glenn Anderson— it sometimes gets overlooked that Lowe holds the Edmonton Oilers' record for most regular-season and playoff games played (1,037 and 172). Only once in his NHL career did his teams miss the playoffs. Lowe also has a trophy named after him in the Quebec Major Junior Hockey League. It goes to the QMJHL player deemed to be the league's best defensive defenceman.

Lowe takes
his man.

★ ★ ★ **Career Highlights** ★ ★ ★

- **Won the Stanley Cup six times, five with Edmonton and once with the Rangers.**
- **Won the King Clancy Memorial Award in 1990.**
- **At the 2002 Olympics in Salt Lake City he served as Assistant Executive Director for the Canadian team that won the gold medal.**

Lowe and friend Wayne Gretzky (back).

For years afterward the Oilers would talk about leaving the arena after the last game and seeing the Islanders quietly celebrating in their dressing room, covered in ice packs, thoroughly drained. It was then that they understood the commitment and sacrifice that went into winning.

In the 1984 finals, the Oilers showed early they had learned about good defence, too, and shut out the Islanders on Long Island, 1–0, in goaltender Grant Fuhr's finals debut. But two nights later it was time for another lesson as the defending champions bounced back with a 6–1 win, sending the series back to Edmonton for the next three games (to avoid excessive travel, the NHL implemented a 2–3–2 playoff system for a short time).

"We returned to Edmonton with a split in the series and knew we would have to play harder. We won games three and four pretty convincingly [both were 7–2 scores]."

That set the stage for game five. It wasn't a must-win situation for the Oilers, but if they lost they'd have to play the final two games on the road and they realized the importance of finishing off an opponent when they had the chance.

"We got out to a four-goal lead after two periods in game five. The Islanders were a proud and powerful team, though, and they didn't quit. They scored two quick goals in the third period to get back in the game, but in the end, obviously, we were able to hold them off. Dave Lumley scored the final goal [to make it 5–2] into an empty net. As I watched the puck slide into the net, time kind of stood still. I will never forget that moment and a million thoughts entered my mind. 'My God,' I thought, 'we are actually going to win this thing.' We just won the Stanley Cup!

"I thought about all the time you play as a kid, all the practices, all the tournaments and the travel that you have to make when you're playing. I thought about the devastating loss to these same Islanders the year before in the finals and now, here I am, being a part of winning something that is the dream of most kids in Canada.

"I was 25 years old when I won my first Stanley Cup. The celebration inside the arena with my teammates was like no other. My family was there, too. It was great to celebrate with them in the dressing room. Like most hockey families, my family sacrificed a lot so that I could play hockey. I was glad that night to be able to share the Stanley Cup win with them.

"I remember, too, that in Alberta in the spring and summer the sun doesn't set until after 10 p.m. You walk into the rink in daylight, you play the game, you leave and it's still daylight. It was a surreal scene that night outside the rink with all of Edmonton celebrating the Cup win.

"Ken Linsemen, Mess, and I left the arena together to head over to a formal function to celebrate the win. I remember all of us saying as we got into my car for the ride over to the event, 'My God, what did we just do? Can you believe we actually did it. We actually won the Stanley Cup?'"

After winning four more times in Edmonton and a decade later in New York, Lowe eventually found his way back to the Oilers.

After retiring he served as an assistant coach, then head coach before taking over from Glen Sather, the architect of those Stanley Cup-winning teams, as general manager of the Oilers. In the summer of 2008, he hired Steve Tambellini as GM and moved up to president of the Oilers.

He scored 19 goals that regular season, a career high. And he scored three more in the playoffs, none bigger or more memorable than the final one.

"My greatest day in hockey was June 7, 1997, the day we won the first Stanley Cup in Detroit. Game four. Literally, because we were up 3–0 in games. Going to the rink knowing you were going to win the Stanley Cup that night, I mean, it was the greatest, most confident feeling that we had."

Although the Red Wings had a stranglehold on the series and their opponent, the Philadelphia Flyers, had been embroiled in some controversy after the third game—coach Terry Murray questioning their commitment to win—they did not want to go quietly into the night in the fourth game. Indeed, although the Red Wings were on the verge of a sweep, the first two games were close, Detroit winning both 4–2, while the third game turned into a 6–1 clobbering after the Flyers had actually opened the scoring.

"The fourth game was a tough game. I was able to score in that game. It was the second goal. The game winner as it turned out. I remember the play. I was coming back on the right wing, coming into the centre. Vlady [Konstantinov] took a hit—I don't know who it was from—but he moved the puck up to Tomas Sandstrom.

"It was a line change and Sandstrom hit me with a pass at centre ice and I had a one-on-one with Janne Niinimaa. I remember I was thinking dump and change, but when I was thinking about dump, he sort of moved to the right and I pull-dragged it around him. I had a step and I remember thinking to myself, 'Oh my God, I've got a step on him!'

"I sort of had my head down as I was leaning because he was sort of diving back and [Flyers' goaltender Ron] Hextall came flying out at me. I actually pulled it around and I remember having the puck in the middle of the paint, so I'm literally like a foot or two feet from the net saying to myself, 'Don't miss the net,' and thankfully I didn't.

"It was one of those surreal experiences. Then I remember I went to crash into the boards and did a pirouette. I remember coming out and seeing Stevie's [Yzerman] face and he was saying, 'What the bleep was that?' And I said, 'I have no idea where that came from, but timing is everything, right?'

"The thing I will always remember is there was a faceoff with about five seconds left outside our blueline. Eric Lindros had just scored to make it 2–1 a few seconds earlier. I was out there with Stevie and Shanny [Brendan Shanahan], Nick [Lidstrom] and Vlady. We won the draw and Vlady shot it down the ice. I knew there were a few seconds left, but I went as hard as I could down the ice because I wasn't going to let anything happen.

"So when the buzzer went I turned around and I had that sort of panoramic view of everything because I was in the other end and I could see everybody coming off the bench. The place was so loud, it was quiet. I remember making the full sprint into the pile, but it was like a sea.

Darren McCarty in his first tour of duty with the Red Wings.

An original member of the Red Wings' "Grind Line" with Kris Draper and Kirk Maltby, Darren McCarty was also an original with the rock band "Grinder." The group was formed in 1997 after the horrible limousine accident in which Red Wings' Vladimir Konstantinov, Slava Fetisov and trainer Sergei Mnatsakanov were severely injured after a team party. On the suggestion of a club trainer, McCarty decided to form a rock band to perform a song on a tribute album— Believing in Detroit: A Tribute to Vladdy and Sergei—that was being made to raise money for the injured. They recorded a single called "Step Outside" with McCarty performing lead vocals. Over the next few years the group performed several shows.

★ ★ ★ Career Highlights ★ ★ ★

- In 1996–97 had a career-high 19 goals and 49 points with Detroit.
- Won the Stanley Cup four times.
- Played his junior hockey with the Belleville Bulls and had 55 goals and 127 points his final season.

McCarty enjoys his day with the Cup in the summer of 2008.

You see those panoramic pictures, everyone going crazy in the stands, emptying the bench.

"To do that and to win after everything we had gone through, losing the year before, losing in the Cup finals in '95, it being the first Cup win in 42 years, up 2–0 going into the third period and it was like that excitement, that nervousness but that excitement of winning, and to be able to do it with those guys, in that city, for every little reason.

"My grandma was there; my dad was still here; I had everybody there celebrating in the dressing room. I wasn't drinking, so when the Cup got passed around to me the guys cleaned it out and put Diet Coke in there. Those little things you always remember. It was so much fun. It was unbelievable. The whole day from start to finish.

"I get chills now just thinking about it and just to be a part of something like that..."

A reliable, hard-nosed third-line winger, McCarty played a valuable role on the Red Wings' Grind Line with Kris Draper and Kirk Maltby. He won a second Cup the following year when Detroit swept Washington and a third in 2002 when they defeated the Carolina Hurricanes in five games.

McCarty in the dressing room.

As a person and a player, McCarty hit rock bottom in the summer of 2007. He played two years with Calgary after the lockout but missed most of the second season recovering from a hernia injury.

That summer he was without a team. Away from the rink, he was struggling, too. He had incurred huge gambling debts, continued to have drinking problems, and was estranged from his family. But one day he realized he needed to get his life turned around and was embraced by his first wife and kids. That fall he started an improbable comeback deep in the minors that eventually led to a return to the Red Wings on March 7, 2008, another great day in his life, and a fourth Stanley Cup in the spring.

"Sobriety, family, and hockey are the three priorities in my life, in that order. When I lifted the Cup, the last year went through my mind. To go from where I was to this moment was incredible."

Marty McSorley

Dad and Son Go Back in Time

There are more than a few moments in his hockey career that Marty McSorley will not forget, some good, some not so good. There was no shortage of success, including two Stanley Cup victories with the Edmonton Oilers and an extended run alongside Wayne Gretzky with the Los Angeles Kings.

There were darker moments, of course, including a year-long suspension and assault charge, for which he was found guilty, for high sticking Donald Brashear during the 1999–2000 season, and an infamous illegal stick penalty in the 1993 Cup finals.

Those moments certainly clouded, but didn't entirely overshadow, a pretty good career for a guy who worked hard and fought hard for everything he achieved. McSorley became one of the top enforcers in the game, fighting for his teammates on the ice and, for a while, fighting for their rights with the players' association off it. In the end, though, his greatest day happened while watching an oldtimers' practice with his father, Bill.

"It would be easy to say my first day in the NHL and my first Stanley Cup, but my greatest day in hockey was during the All-Star Game in Montreal back in 1993. I was there for [NHL Players' Association] meetings. I called my dad—this was after my mom [Anne] had passed away—and I told him to come on up to Montreal and enjoy the weekend and the experience.

"I looked at the schedule for the weekend and saw that the oldtimers were practising and said to my dad, 'Let's go over to the Forum.' So we went over to the Forum and he and I were two of just four people sitting in the stands. Out on the ice skated Red Kelly and John Ferguson and Phil Esposito, so many of these people whom we had watched for years on *Hockey Night in Canada*. Growing up, I'd watch with my nine brothers and sisters, 10 kids [three girls, seven boys]. Mom would make popcorn, and we'd sit around and watch *Hockey Night in Canada,* and we'd go to bed as soon as the game was over."

Indeed, pretty much the only time the kids were allowed to watch TV was when there was a hockey game on. The rest of the time they worked the farm or, in the winter, went skating on the frozen canal where there was often the odd scrap over who in the family got to use the best skates or sticks.

"That day, my dad sat there and he was so excited. He'd be talking about the guys saying, 'This guy did this, he did that. Red Kelly was an all-star defenceman this year and the next year he was an all-star centreman.' He was going on, and he was so excited.

"At that moment, I knew why I was a hockey fan. At that moment, I knew why with 10 kids he really wanted us all to play, or why he would go down and scrape the canal that ran through our farm [in Cayuga, Ontario] with the blade off the back of the tractor, so we could all skate, or to make sure that we all had skates.

"It was why I was a hockey player, or why I loved hockey and it was so much of the fabric of our family. I went away from there [Montreal] and I remember telling my brothers what a great moment it was. To me, thinking back on that, to watch those great players, in the Montreal Forum,

February 5, 1993   Montreal Forum

McSorley chats with a referee.

It was one of those moments that could have happened to anyone. Unfortunately for Marty McSorley, it happened to him. It was late in game two of the 1993 Stanley Cup finals. The Los Angeles Kings had won the series opener and were a few minutes away from taking the second game in Montreal when the Canadiens called for a measurement of McSorley's stick. McSorley ended up having an illegal curve on the stick and received a two-minute penalty. On the ensuing power play, with the goaltender pulled and the Canadiens effectively with a two-man advantage, Eric Desjardins scored to tie the game, 2–2. He then completed his hat trick 51 seconds into overtime to give the Canadiens the win and new life. They never lost again in the series and McSorley never stops hearing about the measurement. Sadly, that call overshadowed a splendid playoff for McSorley. "It was a mistake," he said simply.

Dad and Son Go Back in Time

☆ ☆ ☆ **Career Highlights** ☆ ☆ ☆

- Won two Stanley Cups with the Edmonton Oilers.
- In addition to being tough, he was very versatile, playing defence and wing.
- In 961 NHL games, he had 359 points and 3,381 penalty minutes.

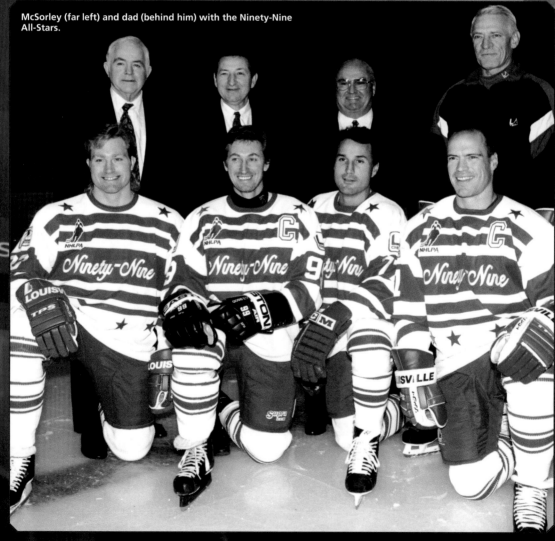

McSorley (far left) and dad (behind him) with the Ninety-Nine All-Stars.

with so few people, sitting with my dad and talking about hockey, was such a precious moment. It was my best day in hockey.

"Over the years, my dad never told me how to play hockey. He made sure we had a rink and equipment as kids, but his line to me was just be a good professional. It was important to him. It was always wear a shirt and tie. When we went to Maple Leaf Gardens, he always wanted to walk around and see the pictures of the guys after they had won the Stanley Cup."

McSorley and his dad created a snapshot like that of their own in 1987 at Northlands Coliseum when the Oilers defeated the Philadelphia Flyers in seven games to win his first Stanley Cup.

"I knew from my mom that he had trouble watching the games, that he would be under the stands walking around. So when we finally won, he came out to where the Zamboni was, standing there by the glass. I went around trying to see where they were in the stands and my dad was standing there by the door. So the doors were opening and I brought him out on the ice. I remember what I said to him: 'Dad, we've got our name on the Stanley Cup.'"

The television cameras that night showed big Bill McSorley, the farmer from Cayuga, with tears in his eyes, being hugged by his son. A few years later, during the NHL lockout in 1994 that spilled into 1995, Marty McSorley managed to steal a few days away from the labour negotiations to hook up with Gretzky and his Ninety-Nine All-Stars tour of Europe.

Bill McSorley had been convinced, literally arm-twisted, by Gretzky to come along. He was torn about a flight to Europe, uncertain about

whether Marty would be able to make it. The fathers of Gretzky, Mark Messier, Paul Coffey, and McSorley were all made assistant coaches to Doug Wilson, though their responsibilities were often little more than ceremonial. Once again the Great One scored, and Bill boarded the plane. A few days later, Marty made a surprise arrival.

"It's really, really special. All those hours you put in, even if you're in the NHL, you're not playing hockey for a pay cheque. You're playing because you really love the game, and you last in the game because you really love to play, and I got that love of the game from my mom and my dad."

After the Oilers won the Stanley Cup in 1988, McSorley received his ring and gave it to his father in appreciation for all he had done and to help him feel a little better because Anne was close to death. She had been diagnosed with leukemia four months after the first Cup win and, sadly, died three months after the second.

When Gretzky's sweater was retired at the start of the 1999–2000 season in Edmonton, Gretzky wanted McSorley to be there that night, just as he had wanted him to be a part of the big trade to Los Angeles in 1988. Ultimately, McSorley knew what his job was and did it very well—having learned from his father, who, as the old tale goes, once shouted at the McSorley's dog after it had ran scared from a coyote on the farm, to "get back in there and fight."

But Marty also got that love and passion for the game from his father, and he realized it that day watching an oldtimers' practice at the Forum.

So Many Moments

Asking Mark Messier to identify his greatest moment in hockey is like asking Tiger Woods to select his favourite major triumph or Steve Nash which of his MVP trophies sits a little higher on the mantelpiece. Does God have a favourite creation day?

Okay, the God analogy is a little much, but when one listens to Messier—arguably the most complete forward to ever play the game—talk about his greatest moment in hockey, well, they do kind of run together.

"There isn't one single moment that I could identify as my greatest. It's literally impossible to pick one best day. There are just too many things that happened over a 25-year career. To pick one would undermine the others.

"As a player I won six Stanley Cups. That is what we play for. That is the intention every year when you start, so to win them is what it is all about. That's the reason you play—to win the Cup. For me there was no other motivation other than to win."

Messier won five Stanley Cups with the Edmonton Oilers' dynasty from 1984 to 1990 and a sixth with the New York Rangers in a now legendary seven-game series with the Vancouver Canucks in 1994. But for Messier there was more to winning hockey than just playing in the National Hockey League, and like his good friend, Wayne Gretzky, he was a fixture in international competition, especially the Canada Cup.

Messier hoists the Cup in 1990 as Oilers' captain.

So Many Moments

The intense gaze of Mark Messier.

His career spanned 25 years and included six Stanley Cup victories and several international successes. He was regarded as not only a great player, but one of the greatest leaders of all time. He helped to lead one franchise to five Stanley Cup wins and helped to end a 54-year championship drought for another. It should come as no surprise then that Mark Messier had his famous number 11 retired by two teams. Messier became just the fifth Edmonton Oiler to have his sweater raised to the rafters of Rexall Place, joining Wayne Gretzky, Jari Kurri, Paul Coffey, and Grant Fuhr. He was also the fourth player to have his number retired by the New York Rangers, joining Rod Gilbert, Ed Giacomin, and Mike Richter in the rafters of Madison Square Garden. Messier wore the number 11 in honour of his father, Doug, who played minor professional hockey. Mark wore it throughout his career, though he briefly wore 27 with Cincinnati of the WHA in his first year of pro.

★ ★ ★ **Career Highlights** ★ ★ ★

- Finished his career with 694 goals and 1,887 points in 1,756 games.
- Won the Conn Smythe Trophy in 1984.
- Won the Hart Trophy in 1990 and 1992.

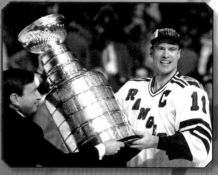

Messier with the Cup as Rangers' captain in 1994.

"As a child what do you want to do? I wanted to get to the NHL and win a Stanley Cup, but I was also able to represent my country in the Canada Cups, including the 1987 series which was one of the greatest series ever. But that is a whole other world."

Messier does have a certain affinity for his first and last Stanley Cup wins simply because there's nothing like winning for the first time. And he did win the Conn Smythe Trophy in that spring of 1984, too. There's also a special memory attached to going to New York to end the Rangers' legendary 54-year Cup drought, a memory which became even more special after Messier's promised victory on the eve of game six of the semi-finals while trailing New Jersey, 3–2, in the series. But Messier made good on the promise, delivering the win with a special performance himself. Always the leader, he led mostly by example.

But he also can't dismiss the other four Stanley Cup wins because each one had a challenge that was unique for its time. "There are so many inner stories to each Cup. It's hard to put one ahead of any other. The first and sixth Cups were very special for all the obvious reasons, but the others were just as magical because of the storylines within the team, the disappointments and the triumphs you go through to get there in the end." One would think winning that last one in Edmonton as captain and without the legendary Gretzky is a special story, indeed.

With six Cups and an impressive 26-year career, one might think Messier would be content to spend his post-career years figuring out which of his many great moments truly was the best of the best, but while he insists he can't rank them, he admits, like Gretzky, that retirement offers an interesting and relaxing perspective on his career.

"I know what Wayne meant when he said his retirement was a great day. It was a time to think back on my career and acknowledge it was a pretty good career. You never allow yourself to do that as a player. You're always looking around the next corner to see what's ahead and trying to figure out how you're going to get there."

Messier has done that since his first ever pro camp, one in which he wasn't very sure he was going to succeed. It was that fear of failure, coupled with a desire to be the best, that drove him through that camp and each one that followed.

"Sure, making it to the league is a great day and I can remember my first camp like it was yesterday, but I couldn't say it was my best day. And once you get there you have to stay there and try to win a Cup. As a player, you don't want to live in the past, just looking back on what you accomplished. You always want to be moving forward and doing better.

"As a player, the six Cups were all great days because that is what we play for. But as a person, the retirement, the induction into the Hockey Hall of Fame, and being able to reflect on those great days was pretty special, too."

Messier, who finished his career with 694 goals and 1,887 points, twice won the Hart Trophy and Lester B. Person Award. Soon after his retirement the NHL introduced the Mark Messier Leadership Award, fitting for one of the greatest leaders in the game.

Draft Promises an NHL Career

Mike Modano or Trevor Linden? That was the question facing the Minnesota North Stars and general manager Lou Nanne on the morning of the 1988 Entry Draft in Montreal.

The North Stars owned the first pick overall in the draft, after finishing the previous season with 19 wins and 51 points, eight points fewer than the Vancouver Canucks, which had the second pick.

It was the third time in their history that the North Stars had selected first overall and they were batting only .500, having taken a bona fide star in Bobby Smith first in 1978 and selecting an eventual journeyman in Brian Lawton in 1983.

So it came down to the top two-ranked junior players: Modano, a slick centre with the Prince Albert Raiders, or Linden, a rugged winger with the Medicine Hat Tigers. Until Nanne walked to the microphone to announce the pick, few knew for sure who would be the selection, least of all Modano.

"The day I was drafted [was my greatest day]. Sitting in the Montreal Forum, knowing the whole wait was about to be over. The only thing was, I didn't know where I was going to be playing. It was nerve-wracking. Minnesota hadn't told me. Lou Nanne said later they hadn't made their decision until 10 o'clock the night before, but they didn't tell me."

Before the selection was made, several trade possibilities had emerged. According to reports of the day, Philadelphia had offered a package of draft

A teenaged Mike Modano with the Prince Albert Raiders.

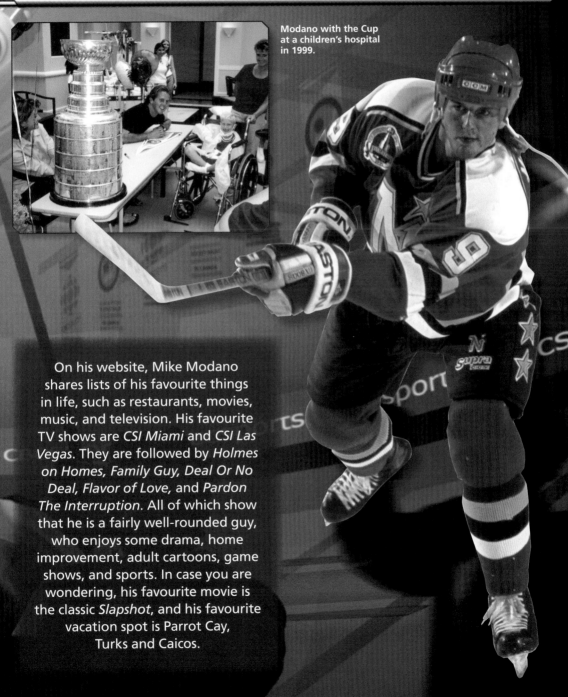

Modano with the Cup at a children's hospital in 1999.

On his website, Mike Modano shares lists of his favourite things in life, such as restaurants, movies, music, and television. His favourite TV shows are *CSI Miami* and *CSI Las Vegas*. They are followed by *Holmes on Homes, Family Guy, Deal Or No Deal, Flavor of Love,* and *Pardon The Interruption*. All of which show that he is a fairly well-rounded guy, who enjoys some drama, home improvement, adult cartoons, game shows, and sports. In case you are wondering, his favourite movie is the classic *Slapshot*, and his favourite vacation spot is Parrot Cay, Turks and Caicos.

★ ★ ★ Career Highlights ★ ★ ★

- Holds record for career goals by a U.S.-born player (528).
- Broke the Stars' club record for total career points (868) on February 14, 2001.
- Recorded his 1,000th career point on November 15, 2002.

Modano with the Dallas Stars.

picks to swap for the first pick. Quebec, which selected third and fifth and wanted Linden, also tried to trade up. All sorts of trade talk occurred, but in the end Nanne couldn't get the package he wanted and the guarantee he would get his man. All that was left was to decide which player to take.

After weighing input from his scouts, Nanne said the belief was Modano had more skills and they needed a talented centre and point producer at the time. Linden, who retired after the 2007–08 season, had a terrific career with Vancouver, the New York Islanders, Montreal, and Washington. He had 375 goals and 867 points. The Canucks insisted afterwards he was the player they wanted, particularly for his leadership.

But Modano, a native of Livonia, Michigan— a factor that also weighed in the North Stars decision—turned out to be the more prolific scorer, exactly what Minnesota needed.

It took several seasons before Modano was able to establish himself as the better player of the two, though. After all, Linden led Vancouver to the Stanley Cup finals in 1994, where the Canucks lost to the New York Rangers in seven games.

Modano with Team USA.

Modano, who helped lead the Stars to a Stanley Cup win in 1999 after the team had moved to Dallas, had 23 points in 23 games that spring. He went on to become the all-time leading scorer among American-born players with 528 goals and 1,283 points. On March 17, 2007, he passed Joe Mullen (502) for the goal-scoring record by American-born players. On November 7, 2007, he passed Phil Housley for the points record. He is the Stars' all-time leader in goals, assists, points, game-winning goals, power-play goals, and shorthanded goals.

During that 1999 playoff run, Modano led all players with 18 assists. He helped get the Stars back to the finals in 2000, but they lost to the New Jersey Devils. Back in 1991 he had helped get the North Stars to the finals but they were easily defeated by Mario Lemieux and the Pittsburgh Penguins.

Modano has also been a fixture in Team USA ventures, playing in the 1990 and 1993 World Championships, as well as the 1998, 2002, and 2006 Winter Olympics.

But it came right down to the last second on June 11, 1988, before he knew where he would be playing. "Now guys know in the morning who is picking them. Or in the NFL, they negotiate weeks before. But I liked it the old way better." It was nerve-wracking, but ultimately rewarding.

By the time the 1984 Entry Draft rolled around, the New Jersey Devils had made it to the Stanley Cup playoffs just once in their first 10 years of existence, and lost in the first round.

After that draft in 1984 they wouldn't make it again for another four years, but they added a key building block. His name was Kirk Muller, a talented forward who called Kingston, Ontario, home but who played junior in Guelph—or, as trivia buffs note, the guy who was drafted second that year behind Mario Lemieux.

"My first seven years playing in New Jersey and being a part of an organization that started off at the bottom was a challenge, but it is nice to see something grow. Lou [Lamoriello] came in and built it up to one of the elite ones now. But having seven years there of growing with guys like John MacLean and Brendan Shanahan and Ken Daneyko, it was such a great part of my career. We were all young, growing together, building together."

In 1988, in fact, four years after Muller arrived, the Cinderella Devils went to the semi-finals and were just one win away from a berth in the Stanley Cup finals before their amazing run ended in a game-seven loss to the Boston Bruins. Three seasons later, Muller was traded with goaltender Roland Melanson to Montreal.

"I had a lot of great memories from back then in New Jersey, but getting traded to Montreal! How fun it was to play in such an exciting city, with the people and the passion for hockey and close to my home and family in Kingston."

The team took a most improbable run to the Stanley Cup in 1993. That season, the Canadiens had a good year, finishing with 102 points, third in their division and seventh overall. But after a perfect February, they struggled down the stretch, winning just four of their final 10 games.

"I look back and think of how much turmoil we had going into the playoffs. We had lost a lot of games those final weeks and we were facing a really strong team in the Quebec Nordiques in the first round. Of course, then there is the pressure in Montreal. A lot of people didn't give us much of a chance against the Nordiques in that first round, and then we went down two to zip." Indeed, the Nordiques won the series opener 3–2 in overtime at home. They won game two more comfortably, 4–1.

"Things certainly didn't go well, but guys like [general manager] Serge Savard stayed really calm through the tough times and made us still believe. There's a funny story. I remember after game two, we went back to get on our plane to go back to Montreal and the plane broke down. I remember going back to the hotel and Serge standing up. We had a team meal, and whether he meant it or not, he said very confidently, 'Hey, guys, if you keep playing the way you are, you will win this series.'

"That one simple message, to me, was important. It really seemed like no one was panicking. We had a good group of guys who battled hard. We won the next four against a really strong team. We realized then we could do it together and play with anybody. We had that momentum and carried on from there."

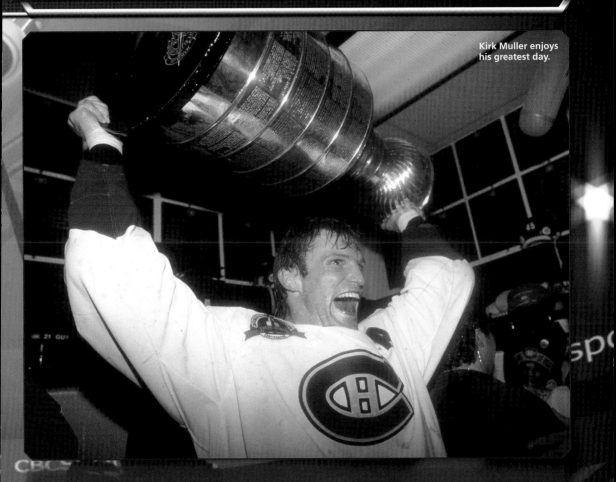

Kirk Muller enjoys his greatest day.

As a player, Kirk Muller never wanted to leave Montreal. But it happened, of course, and he wasn't happy when it did. The Canadiens shocked many, including Muller, when they dealt him to the New York Islanders on April 5, 1995. Muller admitted he felt betrayed, but his heart remained with the Canadiens and he was thrilled in the summer of 2006 when he was added to Guy Carbonneau's coaching staff. He called it a homecoming and Carbonneau said his intention from the day he was named to become head coach was to hire Muller. In preparation for his career in coaching, Muller spent a year coaching at Queen's University, in his hometown of Kingston, Ontario. He was going to return for another season when the Canadiens called. Carbonneau and Muller played together with Montreal when they won the Stanley Cup in 1993.

☆ ☆ ☆ **Career Highlights** ☆ ☆ ☆

- **Earned 959 points over his 19-season career.**
- **Played for Canada in the 1984 Olympics in Sarajevo.**
- **Played in six NHL All-Star Games.**

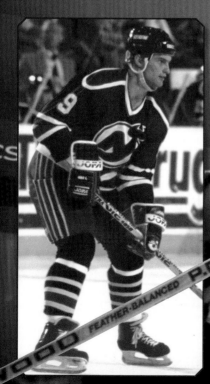

Muller with his original team, New Jersey.

The Habs won that third game 2–1 in overtime, which was significant not only for what it meant in the series, but for what was ahead that spring. After losing the first overtime game in Quebec, they went on to win 10 straight games in extra time, setting a record for most overtime wins in a year and for the most consecutive overtime wins.

The Canadiens swept Buffalo in the second round by four scores of 4–3, then beat a tired New York Islanders team in five before heading to the finals to play Wayne Gretzky and a Los Angeles Kings team that required seven games to beat the Toronto Maple Leafs. The Kings had just three days until the series opener; the Canadiens had an extra five days' rest.

"We had that long break and sometimes you go into a series like that and lose that momentum. L.A. had come off a huge game seven and they beat us in the opener [4–1]. We were losing late in game two, and we knew we had to try something."

That something was the measurement—with 1:45 left in regulation and the Kings leading 2–1—of Marty McSorley's stick.

"In the playoffs, you're always looking for an edge. Early in the game Carbo [Canadiens' captain Guy Carbonneau] and I talked about how illegal his stick looked. At that time we didn't have any thoughts about using it [the rule], but when we were losing, about to go down 2–0 on home ice, the opportunity was there and we said, 'We've got to call this.'"

Defenceman Eric Desjardins tied the game on the ensuing power play with 1:13 left in regulation and won it 51 seconds into overtime, the goal his third of the game. Incredibly, this marked the first time in NHL history that a defenceman scored a hat trick in a Cup finals game. The remarkable run continued with two more overtime wins in Los Angeles, both goals from John LeClair, setting the stage for game five back in Montreal.

"Oh, boy, yeah that was my greatest day. It was the storybook kind of thing. To go into the finals and win the Stanley Cup right in your home rink, just a couple of hours from Kingston, with my family and friends watching. To have the opportunity to score the Stanley Cup-winning goal. It's something you hear many people say, it's true. I can't think of how many times growing up you're pretending with your friends, playing road hockey, that's what you're going to do. When you actually do it, you basically say, 'Hey, my dream just came true.'

"It wasn't the fanciest goal. I can't lie about it. It was early in the second period and McSorley had scored to tie. Basically, Vince Damphousse was playing great at the time. He did some hard work behind the net and like many of my goals, well, they weren't from far out. I figured hey, it's a tight game, if I want to score, go to the net.

"Vince made a great play from behind, getting the puck around. I got into position, quickly jumped on it and got it before Kelly Hrudey was able to stop the second rebound." The goal stood as the winner, the Canadiens ending the series with a 4–1 victory.

"My greatest day was winning the Stanley Cup in Montreal and I was lucky enough to score the Stanley Cup-winning goal and have my family and friends present to witness it and see me the hoisting the Stanley Cup."

Not surprisingly, Bob Nicholson's greatest day in hockey wasn't actually a single day; it was played out over two days.

"Winning the double gold at Salt Lake City in 2002, no doubt about it, were my greatest days. The women won the gold medal on the Thursday, then a few days later the men followed with their win. They were two incredible journeys and to have one foot on each ride was something special."

The Canadian women won their first-ever Olympic gold medal on the heels of a disappointing loss to the Americans in Nagano in 1998, with an inspiring 3–2 victory over the United States.

"The women gave one of the most disciplined performances any Canadian team has ever given. To get through the penalty situation, to show the composure they did and deal with all of the pressure after losing in Nagano, was incredible."

Leading up to the Olympics, the Canadian women had lost all eight exhibition games against the Americans dating back to August 2001. In the gold-medal game, they carried a 3–1 lead into the final period but on the night had to deal with a barrage of penalties. The Canadians were shorthanded 11 times and in one stretch were given eight straight penalties by the American referee, Stacey Livingston.

"The composure was amazing. The officiating was the worst I've ever seen, but the players wanted to win it so badly. I remember flying into Vancouver before the final exhibition game and spending about four hours with Cassie Campbell and Vicky Sunohara talking about the team and the problems it was having. There was dissension with the players and coaches at the time, and they were losing to the Americans. Cassie showed great leadership throughout.

"It wasn't easy, but they dug down and found a way to get it done. It was a tremendous victory. I think it had an impact on the men, too. I remember [men's coach] Pat Quinn was very emotional watching the girls.

Hockey Canada president Bob Nicholson.

Nicholson with the great Hayley Wickenheiser (far right).

After a successful junior career in Penticton of the British Columbia Junior Hockey League, Nicholson played a season of college hockey at Providence. Two of his teammates went on to have prominent careers in hockey, as well. Brian Burke, of course, became a player agent, worked for the NHL, and became a general manager with Hartford, Vancouver, and Anaheim. Ron Wilson was drafted in 1975. He went on to play in Toronto, Minnesota and Europe before turning to coaching. He has been head coach of Anaheim, Washington, and San Jose, and in the summer of 2008 he became head coach of the Maple Leafs. Ironically, Burke was rumoured to be headed to the Leafs as well, while Nicholson had previously been interviewed for the general manager's position in Toronto.

Double Gold at the Olympics

★ ★ ★ **Career Highlights** ★ ★ ★

- **Canada, under Nicholson, is the only country to win double gold in Olympic hockey.**

- **He was inducted into the B.C. Hockey Hall of Fame in 2004.**

- **He has been president and CEO of Hockey Canada since 1998.**

Bob Nicholson (centre) celebrates Olympic gold with Mario Lemieux (right) as Wayne Gretzky shows off the "lucky loonie."

I think our guys got a lot out of that game. I remember Wayne [Gretzky] calling me and saying make sure the girls don't dig up the lucky loonie."

That, of course, was the Canadian dollar coin the Canadians secretly had buried at centre ice for good luck.

It worked its magic again three days later as the men defeated the United States 5–2 to win gold for the first time since 1952. Not unlike the ladies, the men had to deal with considerable adversity along the way. They, too, suffered a disappointing loss in 1998 and finished that tournament in fourth place. At Salt Lake City, it took a while for the team to come together and there was plenty of criticism. They lost their first game, 5–2 to Sweden, then beat Germany by a slim 3–2 score before tying the Czech Republic, 3–3.

In the quarter finals, the Canadians edged Finland, 2–1, then beat upstart Belarus 7–1 in the semi finals before dumping the Americans for the gold.

"When the men lost to Sweden, half the country had broken legs from jumping off the bandwagon. They were losing after two periods to the Finns. It was not an easy ride. If we'd lost that game to the Germans they would have called for another Hockey Summit.

"I remember in that final game, there were about four minutes to go, and I was sitting there with Wayne, Kevin Lowe, and Steve Tambellini. Wayne leaned over and grabbed my shoulder and he said, 'You know Bob, we might have fun in this thing yet.' There was huge pressure on that team to win, but at that moment we could finally feel some relief.

"I'll never forget, after the men won, being in the dressing room. There was all sorts of celebrating on the ice, but in the dressing room it was quiet. There was no media, no family, and the guys just sat quietly in their stalls looking at their medals. There was this great sense of relief and satisfaction.

"I can still see Mario [Lemieux], Steve [Yzerman], and Marty [Brodeur] just sitting there and reflecting on what they had accomplished. That moment was pretty neat. Guys with a cold beer, a few cigars, there wasn't much talking. Just sitting and looking at their medals and feeling good.

"When the women won, it was different. There was a lot of jumping around and yelling. There was incredible pressure on all of those players, and it was two totally different journeys. To see how those two teams came together was pretty special for me.

"One thing I wish I would have done was keep some of the messages I got. After we won, my phone line was plugged. I wish I had kept the recording. I got calls from coast to coast, people yelling and screaming, just so happy. We may have been miles away in Salt Lake City, but we could feel the emotion of the country."

Nicholson played minor and junior hockey in Penticton, B.C. He went on to Providence College and then started his career in hockey administration. He became vice president of the Canadian Amateur Hockey Association in 1989. In 1991, he became senior vice president of the CAHA. In June 1998, he was named president of the Canadian Hockey Association, which later became known as Hockey Canada.

With Nicholson in charge, Canada has once again become dominant in international hockey.

Ed Olczyk

A Goal at Home in Chicago

The old Chicago Stadium was one of the great buildings in all of sport. It was rustic and full of charm. There was a huge organ at one end of the rink and the fans prided themselves on being loud. To play there was something special, especially for a Chicago native.

"Living and dying as a Chicago Blackhawks fan as a kid growing up, to be drafted by them [third overall in 1984] was unbelievable."

Indeed, it almost didn't happen. That year, the Blackhawks owned the sixth pick overall and desperately wanted to select the hometown kid, Eddie Olczyk. The problem was that he likely wasn't going to be available that late. So, Blackhawks' general manager Bob Pulford arranged a trade, moving goaltender Bob Janecyk to the Los Angeles Kings as part of the deal. The teams also flipped first- and seventh-round picks and Chicago tossed in a third-round pick.

The end result was that the Hawks wound up selecting third, but they still traded future considerations to the New Jersey Devils, who were selecting second, and in return the Devils promised not to select Olczyk. The first pick that year was obvious and never in doubt. With it, the Pittsburgh Penguins selected Mario Lemieux. The Devils followed by taking Kirk Muller, leaving Olczyk to the Blackhawks.

A Chicago kid, talented and charismatic, a 1984 U.S. Olympian, he was the perfect fit. His midget team in Chicago won the national title and after a stint playing junior hockey in Stratford, Ontario, he opted to join the U.S. National Team in 1983. He played on the "Diaper Line" with Pat LaFontaine and David A. Jensen on the 1984 Olympic team.

"There wasn't a happier guy in the world than me when I heard them say the 'Chicago Blackhawks select,' and my name was called out. I knew it was probably happening because of the moves being made, but it was still unbelievable. It was a great day.

"But my greatest day, besides winning the Stanley Cup in New York with the Rangers in 1994 and being a small part of it, was my very first game at home in the old Chicago Stadium and scoring a goal. It was October 11, 1984, against the Detroit Red Wings. I will never forget it."

Ed Olczyk

Hockey can be a cruel business sometimes. Players, for instance, get traded and often the move is a huge blow and inconvenience. Take the night Ed Olczyk was traded by the Toronto Maple Leafs to the Winnipeg Jets. "I was in the delivery room with my wife, Diana, who was giving birth to our second child, Thomas. The nurse told me there was a call for me." It turned out to be Maple Leafs' general manager Floyd Smith, delivering the news that Olczyk and winger Mark Osborne had been traded to Winnipeg for defenceman Dave Ellett and winger Paul Fenton. The date was November 10, 1990. "For a lot of reasons I'll never forget that day." The Leafs lost that night, 5–1. On a happier note, Olczyk has managed to score a goal on the days each of his other three children were born.

☆ ☆ ☆ **Career Highlights** ☆ ☆ ☆

- Played a total of 1,031 NHL games and had 794 points.
- Won a national midget title beating a Detroit Compuware team that included Pat LaFontaine and Al Iafrate.
- A top performer for the United States at the 1984 Olympics in Sarajevo.

Olczyk as a member of the New York Rangers.

The youngest player in the NHL that season—just 18 years, 56 days old the night of the first game—Olczyk played on a line with centre Troy Murray and winger Curt Fraser.

"After all those years of sitting in the stands watching and wanting to be a Blackhawk, to be on the ice that night was surreal. There was a reverse dream feel about it. You want it so bad and you just want to get through it. At the same time, it was breathtaking."

And it got even better at the 11:57 mark of the third period. "My first goal. I remember there was a shot from the point. Dave Feamster took it. Troy Murray was going hard to the net. The puck was wide and came off the back boards at a funny angle and I was able to put it in the short side. It was quite the moment. The goalie was Greg Stefan. It was midway through the third period. We went up 6–3 [in a 7–3 win], so it wasn't a big goal in the game, but was a big goal to me.

"After I scored, I got hammered by [Detroit defenceman Doug] Halward on the play. I didn't exactly get to enjoy the moment right away. Keith Brown got the puck for me and I have the puck on the mantle in my home to this day."

Olczyk went on to score 20 goals that season and had 79 points his second season. While happy to play on a Stanley Cup winner, especially since the Rangers won for the first time in 54 years, Olczyk had a small role and appeared in just one playoff game.

Olczyk wound up playing 16 seasons in the NHL, moving from the Blackhawks to Toronto, where he had considerable success. He was eventually traded to Winnipeg—learning of the deal while in the delivery room with his wife—then moved to the Rangers, back to Winnipeg, then to Los Angeles and Pittsburgh, before re-signing with Chicago as a free agent and ending his career there in 2000. He scored 342 goals and had 794 points in 1,031 games.

He went on to work in broadcasting before coaching the Penguins for two seasons. He has since returned to broadcasting, doing national work and colour commentary on local Blackhawks telecasts.

Olczyk playing with the Leafs.

It turns out that one of the greatest hockey players of all time, at heart, is no different than the rest of us.

"I dreamed the same dream as every kid in Canada growing up. You want to be part of a special team, like the one I was involved with in 1970. The dream was to be part of winning the Stanley Cup, and I was fortunate enough to be a part of that. Think about it. Think about all the people who play hockey around the world. There aren't many who get that chance."

Think about all the people who play hockey around the world and there are precious few like Robert Gordon Orr. He is one of a kind.

And he got his chance to be a part of something special in the spring of 1970. He was not just a part of the Boston Bruins playoff success, he was a huge part of their Stanley Cup victory, the team's first in 29 years.

That win, of course, is quite often remembered for not only ending the long Stanley Cup drought in Boston, but for the Cup-winning goal that was scored by Orr, who darted across the

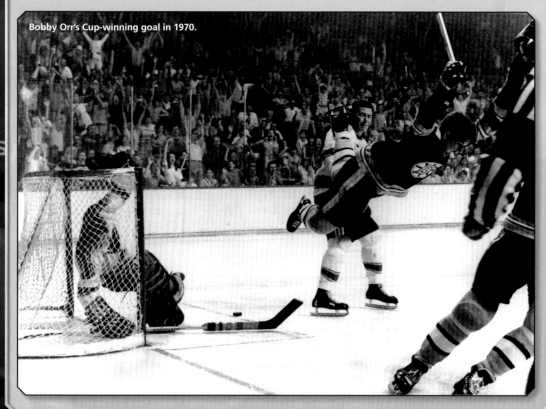

Bobby Orr's Cup-winning goal in 1970.

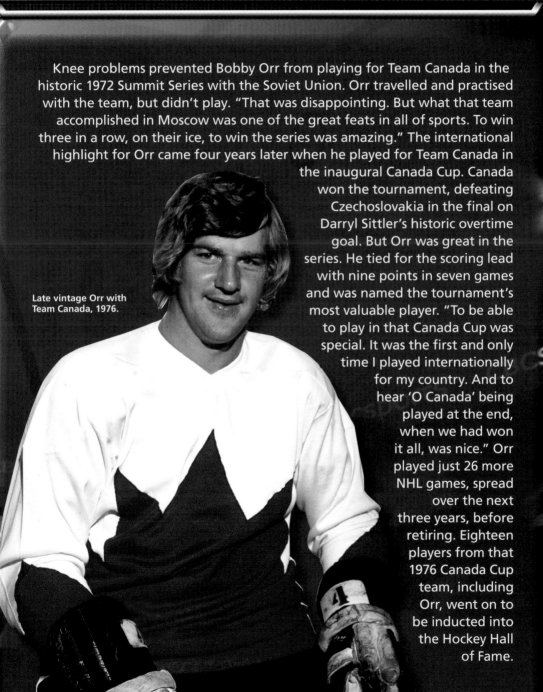

Knee problems prevented Bobby Orr from playing for Team Canada in the historic 1972 Summit Series with the Soviet Union. Orr travelled and practised with the team, but didn't play. "That was disappointing. But what that team accomplished in Moscow was one of the great feats in all of sports. To win three in a row, on their ice, to win the series was amazing." The international highlight for Orr came four years later when he played for Team Canada in the inaugural Canada Cup. Canada won the tournament, defeating Czechoslovakia in the final on Darryl Sittler's historic overtime goal. But Orr was great in the series. He tied for the scoring lead with nine points in seven games and was named the tournament's most valuable player. "To be able to play in that Canada Cup was special. It was the first and only time I played internationally for my country. And to hear 'O Canada' being played at the end, when we had won it all, was nice." Orr played just 26 more NHL games, spread over the next three years, before retiring. Eighteen players from that 1976 Canada Cup team, including Orr, went on to be inducted into the Hockey Hall of Fame.

Late vintage Orr with Team Canada, 1976.

⭐ ⭐ ⭐
Career Highlights
⭐ ⭐ ⭐

- Won the Norris Trophy eight consecutive years.
- Had an assist in his first NHL game against Gordie Howe and the Detroit Red Wings.
- Signed the first million-dollar contract in hockey ($200,000 per year over five seasons).

Orr anchoring the '76 Team Canada blueline.

Orr playing in his first All-Star Game.

front of the St. Louis Blues net, took a centring pass from Derek Sanderson, and while he was being tripped by defenceman Noel Picard, put the puck behind goaltender Glenn Hall just 40 seconds into overtime.

As he scored, to give Boston a 4–3 win and a series sweep, Orr had his arms raised and was flying through the air, propelled by Picard's stick. The picture became one of the most famous and recognizable in hockey.

"That was my greatest day in hockey, but it had nothing to do with the goal. Growing up I always remember watching the Stanley Cup being presented and the captain holding the trophy. When we won it,

Orr's classic goal in 1970 from the end seats.

following Chief [John Bucyk] around the ice, holding the Cup high above his head, well, that was my dream as a kid, to one day be a part of that, and it was happening.

"As a kid, I remember thinking that would be nice if it happened. Life as a professional player is pretty darn good, but that was a great event. That is what you think about when you're playing street hockey, or playing on the bay.

"It was nice to score the goal, but winning was everything. And to know that my dad [Doug] was there made it extra special. He was a big part of the celebration. I remember during the parade he lost his suit coat. He couldn't remember how; he figured he must have given it to someone as a souvenir."

Orr was named the Conn Smythe Trophy winner in that playoff run. He is one of those precious few players who has had an incredible impact on the game. Indeed, it was Orr who changed how defencemen played and how we define the position. Once upon a time, it was mostly about preventing goals, but Orr, on the heels of Doug Harvey before him, made offence as big a part of the responsibility.

In that 1969–70 season, he became the first 100-point defenceman in NHL history. He was the dominant player of his era. He had speed and great strength, a tremendous shot, and was good at both ends of the rink.

He won the Norris Trophy as top defenceman for eight straight years and the Hart Trophy as most valuable player three times. He also led the league in scoring twice, something no defenceman before or since has achieved.

He was the first defenceman to score more than 40 goals in a season (he had 46 in 1974–75) and the first player to earn more than 100 assists in a season (102 in 1970–71). After the Cup win, he enjoyed his most productive season, finishing with 139 points and an incredible plus/minus statistic of plus-124.

Sadly, Orr injured his left knee early in his career. He'd had six operations on it by 1976 and was forced to retire, with two Cup wins to his credit, in 1978. He was inducted into the Hockey Hall of Fame the following year.

Alexander Ovechkin

The Best Is Yet to Come

Ah, let's review the career biography in search of a possible greatest day. He was the first overall pick in the 2004 Entry Draft. In his first season, he had 52 goals and 106 points, tops among all rookies and third best in the league. He became just the second rookie ever to score at least 50 goals, and he won the Calder Trophy. In his first NHL game, he scored twice in a 3–2 win over Columbus.

In his second season, 2006–07, he dipped slightly to 46 goals and 92 points but was still impressive. In his third season he went absolutely crazy. In that 2007–08 season, Alexander Ovechkin led the entire NHL with 65 goals, the first player to reach 65 in a dozen years—since Mario Lemieux—and just one of a dozen ever, setting a new standard for left wingers in the process. He also led the NHL in points (112), power-play goals (22), game-winning goals (11), and shots (446), while finishing ninth in the league with 220 hits. The words "complete package" should be coming to mind about now.

Ovechkin with the IIHF World Championship trophy in 2008.

In the process Ovechkin helped lead the Capitals, who were doormats and dead last in the standings in November 2007, to win 11 of their final 12 games, including the final seven straight, to earn a playoff spot and the Southeast Division title. In his first playoff game, Ovechkin scored the game-winning goal.

When the hardware was distributed in the spring, Ovechkin won the Hart Trophy as most valuable player as selected by the media, the Lester B. Pearson Award as the MVP as selected by his peers, the Art Ross as scoring leader, and the Rocket Richard Trophy for most goals.

No other player has won all four in one season, in part because the Richard has been awarded just nine times—all after Wayne Gretzky and Lemieux retired—and in part because there are few players like this kid.

The Best Is Yet to Come

Ovechkin with the Washington Capitals.

A franchise player since he arrived on the NHL scene, Alexander Ovechkin defies the Russian stereotype of talented but stoic. The kid is as outgoing off the ice as he is all encompassing on it. Quotable, competitive, extremely talented, physically dominant, a team leader, he is the complete package. Not only was he the NHL's Calder Trophy winner in his debut season, but he also made the All-Rookie Team and the First All-Star Team after that 2006 campaign. He's been a first-team All-Star every season since and has won the Hart Trophy (league MVP), Lester B. Pearson Award (MVP as selected by the NHL Players), the Art Ross Trophy (scoring leader), and Rocket Richard Trophy (goal-scoring leader). In addition, Ovechkin has also embraced the league's media blitz, doing league commercials, launching his own clothing line, and enjoying the rivalry (real and concocted) with his Pittsburgh counterpart, Sidney Crosby. He capped it all with a dynamic late-season push, driving the Washington Capitals to the playoffs and the Southeast Division title on the final day of the regular season.

The Best Is Yet to Come

★ ★ ★ **Career Highlights** ★ ★ ★

- **Signed a 13-year contract worth $124 million with the Capitals on January 10, 2008.**
- **Scored the game-winning goal in his first NHL playoff game.**
- **First player in 55 years to be named an NHL first team All-Star in each of his first two full seasons.**

Ovechkin establishes position in the slot.

"It's a big award [the Pearson] because it's who the players think is the best player in the NHL. It means a lot. Everything I have got, I make myself. I'm working hard, and I know it's improving."

Ovechkin is a powerful skater, a deft stickhandler, strong on his skates with a wicked shot, and he gives as much, if not more, than he takes physically. He has been compared, by none other than Gretzky, to Mark Messier, Mike Bossy, and Jari Kurri for his skill set—his toughness, great hands, and quickness. And he is obsessed with being the best and with winning.

"I want to win everything. I want to win games. If I am playing, I want to win."

And he's just 22 years old.

Earlier in his career he twice won gold at the World Junior Championship with Russia and won gold in 2008 at the World Championship after the Capitals had been eliminated from the playoffs. It was Russia's first gold in 15 years.

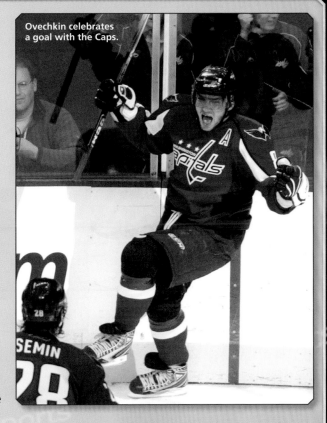

Ovechkin celebrates a goal with the Caps.

He has also already scored what many called one of the greatest goals ever. It happened on January 16, 2006, playing against the Gretzky-coached Phoenix Coyotes. After being knocked to the ice, Ovechkin managed—while rolling over, his back to the net—to slide the puck around the goalie with one hand.

"His future is greatness," said his current coach Bruce Boudreau.

An astute observation, apparently, because despite all that Alexander Ovechkin has accomplished in his young career, from the highlight-reel goals to the gaudy offensive numbers to the improbable run to the playoffs to the sweep of the major awards, he insists the best is yet to come.

Of course there was also signing the 13-year, $124-million contract on January 10, 2008, and receiving the key to the city of Washington after the awards haul, but he is looking forward, not back, for his greatest moment.

"I want to win everything. So next year, maybe the Stanley Cup."

Asked point blank what his greatest day in hockey was, he replied:

"The greatest day of my hockey career is ahead of me."

A Cup for a Kid

The Stanley Cup has a long, rich history of showing up at the strangest times and in the strangest places. There was the time on the beach in Angola, New York, when Barry Smith—a longtime resident of Western New York and, at that time, an assistant coach with the Detroit Red Wings—held a little beach party. Anyone strolling up and down the sands on the southeastern shore of Lake Erie could walk up and touch the Cup as it sat on a picnic table surrounded by beer cans, hot dogs and, as the story goes, a few bottles of bubbly as well.

There's that time when it got a mysterious dent after an all-night party with the Pittsburgh Penguins of Mario Lemieux's era, and that night in Edmonton when it got fitted with a touch of the exotic in a club where the Oilers had taken it dancing (we'll leave the rest to your imagination). And, more recently, the time when Chris Chelios and the Detroit Red Wings had to take it to the repair shop, or so it was reported.

But then there was the day Anaheim Ducks' forward Corey Perry took Lord Stanley's chalice for a hike down Canada's largest and busiest highway.

"My greatest day in hockey was the night that Anaheim beat Ottawa in game five [6–2] to win the Stanley Cup. Lifting the Cup on the ice at the Honda Centre was the thrill of a lifetime for me."

That is to be expected, of course. It is every hockey player's dream come true. And Perry has had no shortage of dream-come-true moments, winning gold with Canada's world juniors and a Memorial Cup with the London Knights in 2005. A first-round pick of the Ducks, 28th overall, in 2003,

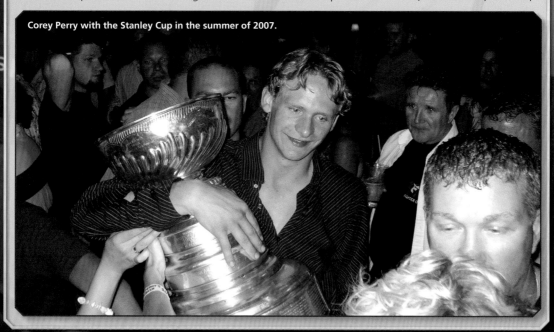

Corey Perry with the Stanley Cup in the summer of 2007.

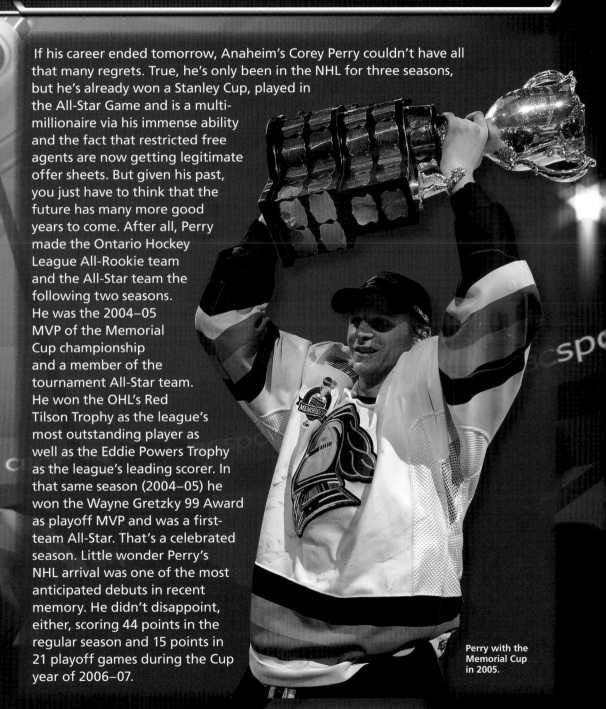

If his career ended tomorrow, Anaheim's Corey Perry couldn't have all that many regrets. True, he's only been in the NHL for three seasons, but he's already won a Stanley Cup, played in the All-Star Game and is a multi-millionaire via his immense ability and the fact that restricted free agents are now getting legitimate offer sheets. But given his past, you just have to think that the future has many more good years to come. After all, Perry made the Ontario Hockey League All-Rookie team and the All-Star team the following two seasons. He was the 2004–05 MVP of the Memorial Cup championship and a member of the tournament All-Star team. He won the OHL's Red Tilson Trophy as the league's most outstanding player as well as the Eddie Powers Trophy as the league's leading scorer. In that same season (2004–05) he won the Wayne Gretzky 99 Award as playoff MVP and was a first-team All-Star. That's a celebrated season. Little wonder Perry's NHL arrival was one of the most anticipated debuts in recent memory. He didn't disappoint, either, scoring 44 points in the regular season and 15 points in 21 playoff games during the Cup year of 2006–07.

Perry with the Memorial Cup in 2005.

☆ ☆ ☆ **Career Highlights** ☆ ☆ ☆

- **Had a career-high 29 goals and 25 assists in the 2007–08 season despite missing 12 games with a deep cut on his leg.**

- **Scored six goals and nine assists in 21 playoff games in 2007 as Anaheim won the Stanley Cup.**

- **Member of Canada's world junior gold-medal winning team in 2005.**

Perry playing for Canada at the World Junior Championship.

he debuted in the NHL for the 2005–06 season, adding another championship to his credit in his second season.

But the story doesn't end there. As every hockey fan knows, each player on the winning team gets a day with the Stanley Cup and Perry wanted to cram in as much as possible in the 24 hours he had with the object of his professional affection. It was August 12, 2007—two months after he got to touch it for the first time.

Perry uncorks the champagne to celebrate Cup victory.

"Lifting it was the thrill, but further to that, spending the day with the Cup…well, we were in [his hometown] Peterborough [Ontario] to show it off to family and friends, and it was a dream come true."

A public celebration was held at the Peterborough Memorial Arena, where Perry signed autographs and posed for pictures with the Cup for several hours.

"After that we had a barbecue at my parents, with family and friends, and we really just enjoyed the day."

The plan then was to take the Cup to London, Ontario, where Perry had won the Memorial Cup with the Knights, to share the fun with old teammates and friends. "We rented a bus and drove the Cup back for another party in London."

But what should have been a three-hour trip turned into a traffic nightmare outside Toronto. "On the way to London, we got caught in traffic because a transport truck was on fire on Highway 401 near Guelph [Ontario] and all lanes were blocked."

According to reports, Perry's bus driver tried to inch his way up the shoulder of the highway but eventually was stopped by a motorist who had pulled over and refused to budge.

"I got tired of waiting on the bus for the traffic to clear up, so I decided to go for a walk on the highway with the Cup. I remember seeing some kids sitting on top of a mini-van and I walked the trophy over to them and let them take their picture with it."

Sure beats wondering, "Are we there yet?"

That family, by the way, was returning home after a day at the Hockey Hall of Fame.

There were more pictures and autographs on the highway, until eventually the traffic cleared and Perry got to London, to a local night spot, where the sharing and the celebration continued.

Two great days with one Cup.

Living Long Enough to Win

Craig Ramsay remembers two days, in particular, during his years in the NHL. One was his greatest disappointment; the other his greatest day in hockey. In many ways, he couldn't have had one without the other.

The first day was when he was relatively young, just 24 years old, in the fourth year of his NHL career. A young but exceedingly talented Buffalo Sabres team had just lost the 1975 Stanley Cup to the Philadelphia Flyers and Ramsay had had enough.

Teammates, media, friends, and virtually everyone he knew and saw told him that it was a tough loss (six games, and then the Flyers parading the Cup on Buffalo ice), but he was young, the team was young and good, and there would be other chances—given the makeup of the team, lots of other chances. Ramsay wasn't so sure.

Craig Ramsay with the Cup in the summer of 2004.

"I remember when we were cleaning out our lockers and I went and stood by the door [where the Sabres always entered and exited the playing surface] and they were breaking up the ice, melting it and washing it down a drain. I don't know why, but it hit me right then. I mean, I believed that we would be back, too, but then I was watching the ice wash away and I remember thinking that not all the guys were young and that maybe, as a team, we wouldn't ever get that chance again."

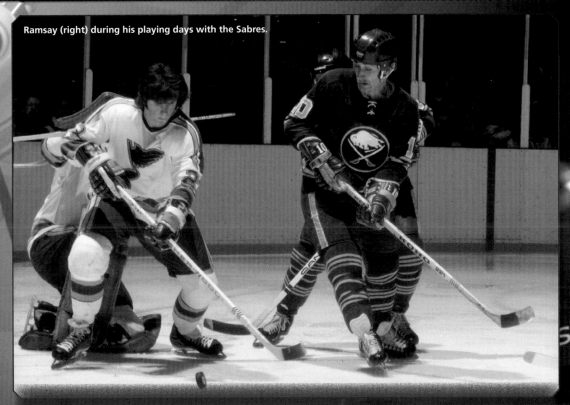

Ramsay (right) during his playing days with the Sabres.

Craig Ramsay was one of the premier defensive forwards in the NHL over a 14-year career that started and finished with the Buffalo Sabres. He earned a Selke Trophy as the league's top defensive forward in what was his last season as a player, but Ramsay had an offensive tick to his game playing on a line with Don Luce and Danny Gare that was considered second only to the famed French Connection in terms of offensive production in Buffalo. In fact, Ramsay was an unappreciated offensive gem for the Sabres, almost always scoring 20 or more goals and ending his career as one of the club's top points leaders. But Ramsay was also an "iron man," playing in 776 consecutive games before being knocked out of the lineup with a broken bone in his foot. It was seemingly part of a legacy from his Peterborough days where iron men like Bob Gainey, Doug Jarvis, and Steve Larmer got their starts. Since ending his playing days, Ramsay has been a coach, a scout, and an administrator in a hockey career that now spans four decades.

★ ★ ★ Career Highlights ★ ★ ★

- **Buffalo's second pick in the 1971 Amateur Draft, he played his entire 14-year NHL career with the Sabres.**
- **His 776 consecutive games-played streak from 1973–1983 ranks fourth overall in NHL history.**
- **Retired in 1985 with 252 goals and 672 points in 1,070 career NHL games.**

Ramsay (left) battles Reg Leach of Philadelphia for the puck.

Craig Ramsay

After a career that saw him play another decade and seldom miss a game, he later became coach and then administrator with the Sabres. During time spent scouting, coaching with Roger Neilson and, for a brief time at least, workng as head coach of the Philadelphia Flyers, that chance never came.

Along the way, he nearly died from a stomach ailment. While on the surgeon's table he was briefly put in a state his doctor told him would deem him clinically dead. It took months to recover from that operation, but with the help of his family, his doctors, and his many friends in hockey, Ramsay did.

He was alive, as well as could be expected, and doing what he always did best after his playing days ended. He was teaching young players how to play. Time passed, but the one goal, the one so many thought was surely in his future, never came.

Finally, 29 springs later, the goal was suddenly, to the surprise of many, achieved. Ramsay was associate head coach to John Tortorella and the Tampa Bay Lightning, and a franchise that had once been the poster team for expansion failure had just defeated the Calgary Flames in a dramatic seventh game on Tampa's home ice. Ramsay's name was going on the Stanley Cup after the Lightning had edged the Flames, 2–1. To do it, the Lightning also had to come back from a 3–2 series deficit and win the sixth game in Calgary, which they did, 3–2, in double overtime.

After the final game—Tortorella at the podium explaining how it all happened and with captain Dave Andreychuk out in the dressing room celebrating with teammates, family, and friends—Ramsay slipped away to the inner sanctum of the coach's office. There, with family and just a handful of very close friends, Ramsay let out a long breath. He sunk contentedly into a chair, and someone handed him a beer.

The celebration was quiet, witnessed by only a precious few, but Craig Ramsay, a one-time Selke award winner and one of the finest defensive forwards the game had known (and capable of some pretty fair offence as well), and the man who had cheated death, had realized his dream.

"I thought back to that day when everyone had told me that it would happen and I remembered thinking that maybe it wouldn't," he said. "I think it was the memory of that day that always kept me going, always drove me to keep chasing the dream. I have a lot of great memories in hockey, and I hope to have a lot more, but I'll never forget that moment in the back room when it finally came to me that it had happened. That was a great moment for me."

Ramsay was more than just a great defensive player. With centre Don Luce and winger Danny Gare they formed a line in Buffalo that shut down the opposition and scored plenty of goals themselves. After 10 straight seasons of not missing a game, Ramsay's iron-man streak ended at 776 games in 1983 when he broke a bone in his foot.

But eventually, in Tampa Bay, the day many said would never come finally did. It was just 29 years in the making.

Mike Ramsey

Do You Believe in Miracles?

Sometimes great moments come so early in a player's career that he tends not to realize just how great the moment until something, or someone, drives the point home.

That happened to Mike Ramsey, a solid defensive defenceman who had a wonderful NHL career with stops in Buffalo (where he was eventually enshrined in the Sabres' Hall of Fame), Pittsburgh, and Detroit (where he was reunited with legendary coach Scott Bowman).

As a coach, Ramsey later returned to the Sabres to be an assistant with his good friend and former teammate Lindy Ruff. Today, he's an assistant coach with the Minnesota Wild in his hometown of Minneapolis, where he grew up in the shadows of the University of Minnesota, his alma mater.

Drafted by the Sabres in 1979, Ramsey played 18 NHL seasons but never won a Stanley Cup. The closest he came was with Bowman and the Detroit Red Wings, losing in the finals to the New Jersey Devils in 1995. The silver

Mike Ramsey during the Miracle on Ice game in 1980.

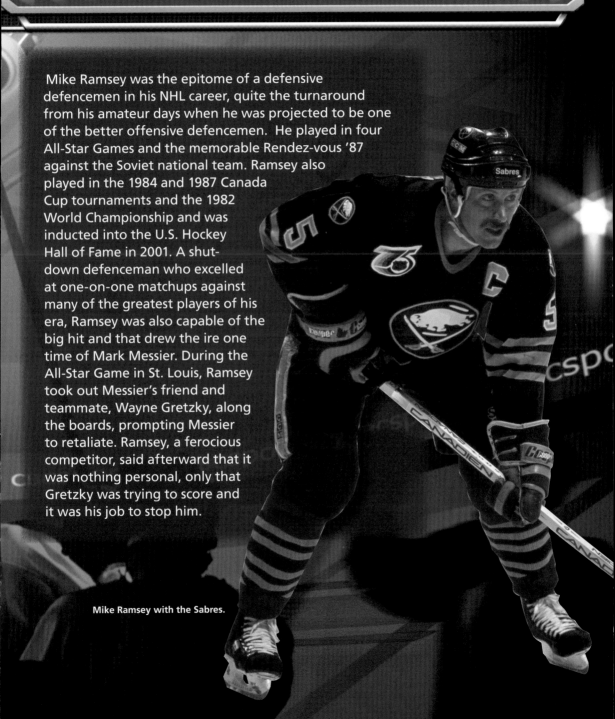

Mike Ramsey was the epitome of a defensive defencemen in his NHL career, quite the turnaround from his amateur days when he was projected to be one of the better offensive defencemen. He played in four All-Star Games and the memorable Rendez-vous '87 against the Soviet national team. Ramsey also played in the 1984 and 1987 Canada Cup tournaments and the 1982 World Championship and was inducted into the U.S. Hockey Hall of Fame in 2001. A shut-down defenceman who excelled at one-on-one matchups against many of the greatest players of his era, Ramsey was also capable of the big hit and that drew the ire one time of Mark Messier. During the All-Star Game in St. Louis, Ramsey took out Messier's friend and teammate, Wayne Gretzky, along the boards, prompting Messier to retaliate. Ramsey, a ferocious competitor, said afterward that it was nothing personal, only that Gretzky was trying to score and it was his job to stop him.

Mike Ramsey with the Sabres.

★ ★ ★ Career Highlights ★ ★ ★

- **Played 18 seasons in the NHL, 14 of them with Buffalo, and made the playoffs in 15 seasons overall.**

- **Member of the University of Minnesota 1979 NCAA championship team and 1980 U.S. gold-medal Olympic team.**

- **Played in four NHL All-Star Games (1982, 1983, 1985, and 1986) and Rendez-vous '87.**

The Miracle on Ice celebration, February 22, 1980.

mug was never his to hold, which was a disappointment, but he did get his hands on precious gold, which represents his greatest day. And it was only because he put his NHL career on hold for a year that he won his Olympic medal.

Ramsey won his in spectacular fashion, as a 19-year-old playing defence for the 1980 U.S. Olympic team that performed the Miracle On Ice in Lake Placid, New York. The upstart Americans, mostly college kids, were given no chance of winning a medal, let alone beating the Big Red Machine that was the Soviet Red Army team in their second-to-last game of the tournament. Outplayed and outshot and trailing 3–2 after two periods, the Americans tied it in the third, and then captain Mike Eruzione scored the winner on a wrist shot midway through the final period. As the seconds wound down, ABC's play-by-play broadcaster Al Michaels gave the unforgettable call:

"Eleven seconds. You got 10 seconds, the countdown going on right now. Five seconds left in the game! Do you believe in miracles? Yes!"

But the Americans still had to beat Finland in the final game for the gold medal. They trailed that night, 2–1 after two periods, but coach Herb Brooks reminded them between periods that they would never forget this day, win or lose. And so they scored three times in the third to win an improbable gold medal.

Beating the Soviets was among the most memorable moments in the history of sport and one that Ramsey can never forget. It was a miracle in many ways. But there was still more work to be done and the miracle would mean nothing without another win. Winning the gold, that was another special moment.

"We were all just standing there after we won and Mike [Eruzione] was standing there when the anthem started. He was on the podium, the top tier and we all had our medals around our necks and the music starts and he just turns to us and says, 'Come on, guys,' and so we all rush up and climb on to it and it's small so were just hugging and holding on to each other and it was an amazing moment."

So too was what happened afterward.

"We go back to our locker room and we realize, that's it. But we didn't know what to do next. We had been staying in a house up on a hill [in Lake Placid] and there wasn't any bus or anything, so we just packed our bags and went out. I was walking up the hill and I had my bag and my sticks and everything and a cop, I think it was a state trooper, comes along and he stops me.

"I mean, I'm 19, I'm just a kid and I guess he thought I was stealing the stuff because I'm all by myself and I've got this Team USA logo all over my bag and everything, but I didn't have any ID with me.

"So I can tell he doesn't believe me when I tell him I'm a part of Team USA and then he asks for ID and I didn't have any, so I pulled out the only thing I had. I figured, hey, I just won a gold medal and I was still wearing it around my neck and I remember asking him, 'Will this do?'

"He said: 'Yeah, go ahead, and congratulations.' I don't think I've ever had a day like that since, and I doubt I ever will."

Gary Roberts

Only Non-Montreal Cup at the Forum

He is fast becoming the grand old man of hockey, a Gordie Howe of sorts for a younger generation—stops all over the hockey map, a never-quit attitude wherever he goes, tough and talented, a great leader and a winner.

At age 42, Gary Roberts is something of a legend in the National Hockey League, the kind of guy you love to have on your team, especially come playoff time. There have been many memories, but Roberts spends a reasonable amount of his reflective moments thinking about his Bryan Adams days, what he calls the best days of his hockey life.

"Without a doubt, my greatest day in hockey was winning the Stanley Cup in 1989 as a member of the Calgary Flames in the Montreal Forum."

He was just a kid back then, having turned 23 a couple of days before that final game, playing in only his third full professional season. It was a dream come true, of course. He was playing on a line with his childhood friend, Joe Nieuwendyk, and with his idol, Lanny McDonald.

Young Gary Roberts with Calgary's Cup in 1989.

Take a look at Gary Roberts' resume in the NHL and you might think he was a useful journeyman— given that he has played for Calgary, Carolina, Toronto, Florida, and Pittsburgh and, starting in 2008–09, Tampa Bay—but nothing could be further from the truth. Roberts is simply one of those sought-after players who makes everyone around him better. It's a legend he developed in his early days as a 50-goal scorer, but one he perfected as his scoring skills started to fade but his knowledge, experience, and amazing dedication to fitness developed. Roberts is a team guy with a tremendous physical game and a dedication to preparation that younger players can't help but notice and, if they are smart, emulate. Cursed with a variety of injuries—including a broken bone in his neck that almost ended his career, and a broken leg after which he refused to be carried off the ice, preferring instead to leave under his own power— Roberts has played almost 1,200 games, a testament to his longevity as well as his ability.

Roberts with the Flames.

★ ★ ★ **Career Highlights** ★ ★ ★

- Won the Masterton Memorial Trophy in 1996.
- Career-high 53 goals in the 1991–92 season.
- Recorded 19 points in 19 playoff games with Toronto in 2001–02.

Roberts with Carolina.

"Both Joe and I idolized Lanny McDonald when we were kids. When Joe and I played minor hockey in Markham [outside Toronto], we watched Lanny play all the time when he was a Leaf. To get to play with Lanny and watch him, to learn from him and experience what he was experiencing during that Stanley Cup drive was storybook."

It wasn't difficult to see why. While Nieuwendyk and Roberts were kids in the spring of '89, McDonald had been playing for 16 seasons, and was in what everyone was pretty sure was his final season. It was now or never for the veteran.

McDonald, who broke in with the Maple Leafs in 1973, was 36 that spring, and pretty much at the end of the line. But in that fateful game on that fateful night—and in the Montreal Forum, no less—the sixth game of the final, McDonald scored a goal to help win the Stanley Cup for the Flames.

Talk about coming full circle. Roberts watched on television when McDonald scored his first-ever NHL goal—in the Montreal Forum. In 1989, he was his teammate and he was alongside when McDonald scored his last one. The achievement, and all that went into it, was not lost on Roberts.

"For the young players on the Flames, Lanny set the tone on and off the ice. To see him finally win that trophy left a mark on me. Lanny McDonald, his heart, his will to compete, his drive, is a big reason why I still play the game today. I always remember Lanny telling me, 'Gary, play as long as you can. There is nothing better than being a hockey player.'"

Roberts obviously took the advice to heart. He played 10 seasons in Calgary before missing a full year because of a neck injury. He returned to play three seasons in Carolina and four more years with his hometown Leafs— wearing his hero's number 7, and reunited with Nieuwendyk, with whom he had played minor hockey and lacrosse in the Toronto area as a teen.

There was a stop in Florida after that, then Pittsburgh where he helped lead the Penguins to the Stanley Cup finals in the spring of 2008, only to lose in six games to Detroit. Appropriately, on the eve of that series, Roberts told the story about winning his first Stanley Cup.

"I was 23 when I won the Stanley Cup in Calgary," he said. "I remember saying, 'How many more of these am I going to win?' Well, I've waited 19 years to get back to the Stanley Cup final."

At least he got his early, unlike McDonald, who had to wait until the final game of his career. In the summer of '08, Roberts signed with the reinvigorated Tampa Bay Lightning, following McDonald's advice to keep playing.

Should the Lightning make it to the Stanley Cup finals and win it all at the end of the 2008–09 campaign it will be 20 years since Roberts saw McDonald live the dream to its end. And you can be sure there will be some young kid thinking the same thoughts about Roberts as Roberts felt about McDonald that May day in Montreal, when the Flames became the only team other than the Canadiens ever to win a Stanley Cup in the Forum.

When you think of all the places he's played and all the pain he's endured to keep playing, it seems only fitting that he give it one more try. After all, like Lanny said, what's better than being a hockey player?

Larry Robinson

Cup as Coach Even Sweeter

In his illustrious 20-year career as one of the best defenceman ever to play the game, Larry Robinson never missed the playoffs. In six of those years he helped lead the Montreal Canadiens to Stanley Cup victories, including four straight with those incredible teams of the late 1970s. He won the Conn Smythe Trophy in 1978, but it was the eighth Stanley Cup ring he earned that ultimately proved to be the most special.

"Considering how long I played hockey and how many Cups I got to win as a defencemen with Montreal, it was my first Stanley Cup win as a head coach that is actually my greatest day in hockey."

Robinson, selected 20th overall by the Canadiens in 1971, won a Calder Cup with Nova Scotia in the AHL before joining the Canadiens, winning his first Stanley Cup as a rookie in 1973. The Canadiens won four more before the decade was over with a dominant team, one for the ages, from 1976–79. Robinson won again, his last time with the Canadiens, in 1986.

"What a thrill it is to be a player who wins the Stanley Cup. To be on the ice in your equipment, the game has just ended and you now have the opportunity to skate around with that trophy.

Devils' coach Larry Robinson with his Cup in 2000.

Robinson back home on the farm with the Cup.

You could call Larry Robinson a two-sport athlete. When he wasn't playing or coaching hockey, Robinson was often involved in polo. Not water polo, rather the polo played with a horse and a mallet. Robinson owned a half-dozen polo horses at one point and actually broke his leg in the summer of 1989 playing polo, while he was still with the Canadiens. Robinson grew up on a farm in Ontario, near Ottawa, but wasn't, as he put it, a natural on horses of any kind, though he loved them. Along with Canadiens teammate Steve Shutt and a veterinarian friend, they helped to form the Montreal Polo Club.

★ ★ ★ **Career Highlights** ★ ★ ★

- Played 20 seasons in the NHL, finishing with 208 goals, 750 assists, and 958 regular-season points.
- Had an additional 144 points in 227 playoff games.
- Played left wing and centre for part of his junior career.

Robinson with the Cup as a player with the Canadiens.

The feeling is almost indescribable. To win the trophy as a coach, though…wow."

Robinson played 17 seasons with the Canadiens and three more with the Los Angeles Kings, twice winning the Norris Trophy. He retired after the 1991–92 season. In 1993, he was named as an assistant coach with the New Jersey Devils. They won their first Stanley Cup in 1995. After that win, Robinson became head coach of the Kings, a job he held until the end of the 1998–99 season when he returned to the Devils again as an assistant coach.

Robinson was named head coach of the Devils with just eight games remaining in the 1999–2000 season, when he was asked to replace head coach Robbie Ftorek, as general manager Lou Lamoriello tried to light a fire under his club before the post-season. It worked.

That spring, the Devils swept the Florida Panthers in the first round, then beat the Toronto Maple Leafs in six games before advancing to the conference finals with a thrilling seven-game victory over the Philadelphia Flyers, in which the Devils had to overcome a 3–1 series deficit.

That series will always be remembered for the amazing comeback, but also for the crushing hit Devils defenceman Scott Stevens administered on Flyers star Eric Lindros early in the final game, leaving him concussed yet again.

In the finals, the Devils led Dallas 3–1 in the series, but the Stars battled back with a 1–0 triple overtime win to force a sixth game. Four of the final five games were decided by one goal, but on that final steamy night in Dallas, centre Jason Arnott scored in double overtime to give the Devils the Cup win.

"It also happened to be the night that my first grandson, Dylan, was born. It was the perfect night. When I think about the countless hours of sleepless nights as a head coach, when I think about the video tape that myself and my assistants Bob Carpenter and Slava Fetisov poured through to find holes in other team's structure, to change things within our own team and to make our players better prepared, all that work paid off with the Cup win.

"When you are a player, you only have to worry about one thing—playing your game. I left the game at the rink when I played. When you're a coach, though, your job consumes you. You're in charge of the entire team. That night was a great night for everyone. But there was a real sense of great satisfaction accomplishing that feat as a head coach."

After leading the Devils back to the Cup finals the next spring, and losing to Colorado, Robinson was fired the following season. He came back a few years later to replace Pat Burns, who was battling cancer. As fulfilling as it was to win as a head coach, the job was, as Robinson conceded, consuming. It also became debilitating. The stress was becoming too much and he stepped down.

Robinson was tough and talented as a player, a great defender but also gifted offensively. Beyond his success on the ice with the Canadiens, he played for Team Canada in the 1976, 1981, and 1984 Canada Cup tournaments. He was inducted into the Hockey Hall of Fame in 1995 and had his number 19 retired by the Canadiens on November 19, 2007.

Getting the Call to Officiate

Ray Scapinello

The last place Ray Scapinello thought he would ever wind up was the National Hockey League.

"I was 20 years old and I had finished playing Junior C hockey in Guelph [Ontario]. When you're 20 years old, playing Junior C hockey, or whatever, you know you're not going anywhere, so you might as well give up the game.

"I was working at Canadian General Electric at the time in their production control department. I was no good at what I was doing. Luckily, a gentleman by the name of Mel McPhee, who happens to be [NHL referee] Bill McCreary's father-in-law, was a member of the Guelph Referees' Association and he said to me, 'Scampi, why don't you join and stay involved in the game?' The NHL was the furthest thing from my mind. But I joined, doing minor hockey games, six, seven, eight games on a Saturday."

Scapinello eventually refereed junior games as well for a couple of years and attended Bruce Hood's officiating school in 1968. After a while, he caught the notice of the NHL, though he went through a tryout camp once and didn't make it and wasn't hired until his second attempt. He was hired by the NHL prior to the 1971–72 season.

"It was Frank Udvari [former referee and officiating director] who found me. I credit my whole career to former referee-in-chief Scotty Morrison. Three years after Mel convinced me to take up officiating, I was a National Hockey League linesman.

"My greatest day in hockey was the day I got hired in 1971 by Scotty Morrison. I signed for the grand total of $6,500. I remember it was at the offices in Rexdale, near the airport. I'm sure I would have signed for free, being so vertically challenged, 5-foot-7 on a good day. But Scotty took a chance on me, and I will always be appreciative of that."

Scapinello early in his career, getting ready for a faceoff.

During his 33 years as an NHL linesman, Ray Scapinello never missed a game. But he came close one night. Scapinello had returned home to the Toronto area during a break in his assignments. He was scheduled to resume work in Long Island for a game between the Maple Leafs and Islanders. Rather than fly to New York the night before, he decided to fly on game day to LaGuardia airport. Trouble was, the weather wasn't co-operating and the flight got sent back to Toronto. From there, Scapinello was eventually able to get a flight into Philadelphia and drove up to New York, arriving late, but arriving nonetheless. "I went out in the middle of the game, switching with [referee] Richard Trottier, who was working the lines."

Getting the Call to Officiate

Scapinello and Wayne Gretzky at the blueline.

Scapinello worked his first NHL game on October 17, 1971, the Minnesota North Stars playing the Sabres in Buffalo. But it was his second game that he remembers most.

"I'll never forget it. I was in Chicago working the game. Buffalo was in playing the Blackhawks. The Sabres were leading 2–1 late in the third period when they dump the puck down the ice. They try to make a change, but Chicago got the puck up the ice quickly. The one defenceman who tried to get off turns and stays on the ice. Another defenceman jumped on, but jumped back off.

Scapinello jumps on the dasher.

"Here I am, game two in my career, a rookie linesman and I call Buffalo for too many men on the ice. Punch Imlach was coaching the Sabres at the time and he was livid. He refused to put a player in the penalty box. Art Skov was the referee and he says, 'Punch, you're on the clock. Get somebody in there.' Punch tells him it was the worst call he'd ever seen and refused to put somebody in. So Skov gave him a bench penalty.

"Now they're two men short and Bobby Hull scores two goals, and the Blackhawks win. The next day in the *Chicago Tribune*, the headline reads: 'Scapinello, Hull beat Sabres, 3–2' and Punch is quoted as saying, 'I don't know who this guy is, but I'm going to find out.' My next game was in Oakland and when it's over the Seals' coach, Vic Stasiuk, was down kicking on our door complaining about me missing an offside call on a goal. I figured I'd never make it past my third game."

Thirty-three years later, Scapinello had worked a record 2,500 regular-season games and 426 playoff games. He worked 20 Stanley Cup finals, three NHL All-Star Games, and the 1998 Winter Olympics in Nagano, and was 20 times voted best linesman in the league.

His last NHL game was April 2, 2004, at age 58, back in Buffalo, the Sabres playing the Maple Leafs. Over those remarkable record 33 years and 2,926 games, Scapinello never missed a single assignment, though there were close calls related to weather and travel problems. In 2008, Scapinello became the 15th inductee into the Hockey Hall of Fame in the officiating category.

"That would be the next greatest moment in my career. It's funny, as an official you spend your entire career trying not to be noticed, but this is one time when it's quite alright. I remember back when I got hired, Scotty telling me the story about [NHL president] Mr. [Clarence] Campbell asking him why he is hiring all these little guys? Scotty Morrison says, 'Mr. Campbell, I've got a good feeling about this guy. He'll be okay.' Thirty three years later, after all those games, I guess he was right. I was just lucky to be in the right place at the right time. It was a great ride."

Savouring the Spoils

It was the spring of 1990 when the Edmonton Oilers won their last Stanley Cup. It's not because it was the last (who knew at the time?), or because they managed to do it without Wayne Gretzky that made it the greatest day for Craig Simpson. That was only part of it. For him it was the journey, and truly soaking up the moment.

On May 24, 1990, the Oilers—led by captain Mark Messier in the second season after Gretzky had been traded to the Los Angeles Kings—finished off the Bruins in five games in the Stanley Cup final, comfortably winning the final game in Boston, 4–1. That spring, Simpson, playing on a line with Messier and Glenn Anderson, led all playoff scorers with 16 goals and 31 points in 22 games.

"Winning the Stanley Cup in the famous Boston Garden, the smallest dressing room in the league, spending a moment with your teammates at the end of a long, difficult journey that is the Stanley Cup playoffs. That is what I remember, that was my greatest day in hockey.

"Getting a chance to sit down, with your back against the cold wall, and look at your teammates, the looks on their faces and the enjoyment that is in the room, and staring at the Stanley Cup and just taking inventory of how you feel. Your body is aching after playing over 80 games and then another 20 or so in the playoffs, pushing yourself to the limit physically. Feeling exhausted, bruised, beaten, but exhilarated all at the same time.

"I can remember that moment like it was yesterday. I can remember the smells. I can remember the sounds. I can remember what everybody looked like and the emotion that was in that room. I purposely took a moment there and I said I want to remember that feeling because that's why you played hockey."

Not many words were spoken, either. On the tape player, Tina Turner's song "Simply The Best" played in the room.

"Guys were dancing around with the Cup. It's the great moment when everyone's gone from the room and it's just you and your teammates. To me it represented everything that is about being a team. You are an individual who relies on other individuals to have success and when that happens, you are a great team.

"In those moments, nobody needs to say anything. It's the rush of emotion and exhilaration that just flows out of you when you win. When you look at the explosiveness of when that clock ticks to zero, the guys jumping off the bench, mauling each other and jumping each other. There is an unspoken energy that happens at that point."

And when it is over, despite the joy, sometimes it is difficult to see it end.

"There's a huge sense of relief when it's over. I always said that if somebody said, 'Oh, we've made a mistake; we've got to play another game,' none of us could because mentally you've gone over that edge already and you couldn't possibly bring it back."

Ironically, the Oilers almost had one of those moments. It happened two years earlier in the same Boston Garden. They were leading the final 3–0 that spring. In the fourth game they were tied

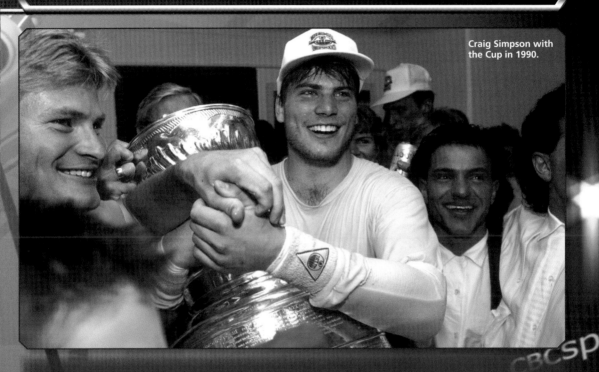

Craig Simpson with the Cup in 1990.

It was an hour or so after the Edmonton Oilers had won the Stanley Cup in 1990. Craig Simpson had celebrated with the masses and had the special, private moment with his teammates. Then he wandered into the hallway in the Boston Garden, just outside the Oilers dressing room, and he saw the legendary Gordie Howe. Simpson, carrying the Cup, walked over to Howe to have a word. "I placed the Cup down and shook Mr. Howe's hand. I could see a look in his eyes, similar to what I was feeling in my heart. With the sight of the Stanley Cup, the smell of sweat and champagne, the buzz of the players celebrating in the background, he was reliving some of his favourite memories. I passed him the Cup, and instantly we looked for his name. Four times it was engraved in the silver, and immediately his eyes went to 1955, the last time in his career that he won. Like it was yesterday, Mr. Howe talked through every game, recounting big goals and key moments in the series and remembering how he felt in the 3–1 Wings victory in game seven over the Montreal Canadiens. That is a moment I will always remember, and truly exemplifies how the Stanley Cup connects generations of players and fans alike."

★ ★ ★ **Career Highlights** ★ ★ ★

- Selected second overall by Pittsburgh in the 1985 Entry Draft.
- Served as an assistant coach with the Edmonton Oilers for two seasons.
- Traded to Edmonton by Pittsburgh as part of a package for Paul Coffey in 1987.

Simpson looking for room in front of the Boston goal.

Craig Simpson

3–3 when the power went out at 16:37 of the second period. The date was May 24, 1988. They were forced to replay the fourth game two days later in Edmonton, the Oilers winning 6–3.

But after winning in 1990, after the moments to celebrate and reflect with his teammates were over, Simpson felt a strange and different emotion.

"That year, I actually felt kind of depressed that it was over. As exhilarated as you were in winning, I was playing the best hockey of my life, at the most important time in my life. I was a little sad that it was over. It took a couple of days despite the excitement of getting the Cup. Part of why you play is because you love playing the games, and I didn't want that to end.

"I remember talking to my dad two or three days later and I said I don't know what I'm feeling, but there's just a pit there that I just wish we could still be playing. Part of you feels… for me personally, I thought I might not ever get to that level of playing again, where everything is just right. The team is right, the line is clicking, and I'm playing my best. I led the playoffs in scoring that year. Going to the rink was just a pure joy. Playing at that level was so exciting.

"Yeah, I know we've got the Cup, but I loved the journey. I didn't want the journey to end. Mind you, I didn't want to take the chance of going to game six and seven, either. The thing that emotionally stands out for me in that final game is sitting on the bench, looking at Mess and Andy. The play is going on, the seconds are ticking down. We took our gloves off, dropped our sticks and just hugged and looked into each other's eyes and knew we've all paid the price to do what we needed to do to win. That's another great moment of sharing with teammates."

Interestingly, it was the second Cup that he appreciated more.

"It was more unexpected. Our team really came together at the right time. And I had met my wife-to-be by then and had someone to share it with. The first Cup was such a blur in many ways. This one I really wanted to soak it all in, and I did."

Darryl Sittler

Tearful Banner Raising

It was 27 years and one day after Darryl Sitter had one of the greatest nights in hockey history that he had his greatest day.

It was back on February 7, 1976, of course, that Sittler, then captain of the Toronto Maple Leafs, had a remarkable night in an 11–4 victory over the Boston Bruins. Sittler scored six goals on goaltender Dave Reece and added four assists, the 10 points in one game an NHL record.

He had two assists in the first period, three goals and two assists in the second, and three more goals in the third period. That year, 1976, was incredibly special for Sittler. That spring, on April 22, 1976, he tied a playoff record when he scored five goals in a game against the Philadelphia Flyers. That fall, on September 15, he scored the memorable overtime winning goal against Czechoslovakian goaltender Vladimir Dzurilla to give Team Canada a victory in the final of the inaugural Canada Cup.

But none of those moments, or his induction into the Hockey Hall of Fame in 1989, or his son being drafted seventh overall by the Flyers in 1992, rank as his greatest day.

Sittler had 389 goals and 916 points in a dozen seasons with the Leafs and was the franchise's all-time leader in both categories until he was passed by captain Mats Sundin during the 2007–08 season.

"It's hard to pick one day. I was fortunate to have a lot of highlights in my career. But the night that stands out for me was

Darryl Sittler (right) and son Ryan watch as Darryl's number 27 is raised to the rafters of the Air Canada Centre on February 8, 2003.

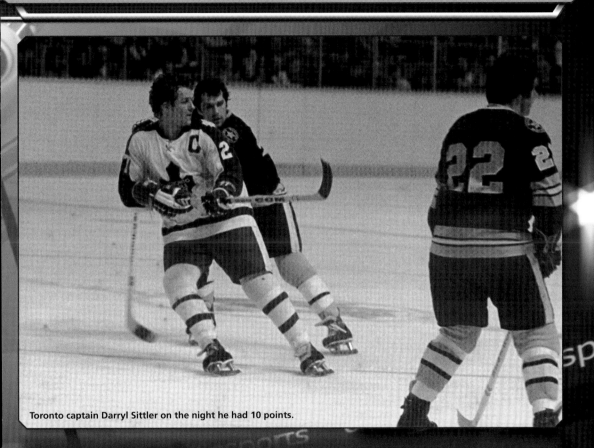

Toronto captain Darryl Sittler on the night he had 10 points.

Of the many accomplishments in his career, one that stood out as among the very best was the day Darryl Sittler was named captain of the Toronto Maple Leafs. Just 10 players had been captain of the Leafs prior to Sittler—Hap Day, Charlie Conacher, Red Horner, Syl Apps, Bob Davidson, Ted Kennedy, Sid Smith, Jimmy Thomson, George Armstrong, and Dave Keon. Sittler took over from Keon as captain in 1975 and wore the "C" officially through to the 1980–81 season. But the thrill died on December 29, 1979, when Sittler removed the "C" from his sweater in protest of the trading of linemate and friend Lanny McDonald by the late Punch Imlach, who seemed intent on picking a fight with his best player. Sittler again wore the "C" after a meeting with owner Harold Ballard, but it was never the same. He was eventually traded to Philadelphia,

Tearful Banner Raising

⭐ ⭐ ⭐ **Career Highlights** ⭐ ⭐ ⭐

- Became captain of the Maple Leafs at age 24.
- Selected a second team All-Star in 1978.
- Son, Ryan, was a first-round pick of the Philadelphia Flyers.

Sittler during the 1976 Canada Cup.

February 8, 2003. It was the night I was honoured by the Maple Leafs and my banner was raised at the Air Canada Centre. It was my greatest day. It was special to be recognized for my career. It's the greatest honour a team can give you. But there was a human side to it, as well."

The banner was supposed to have been raised on October 3, 2001, along with one for Frank Mahovlich, who made number 27 famous before Sittler did. But at the time, Sittler's wife, Wendy, was gravely ill. She had been battling colon cancer for several years and Sittler asked the Leafs to postpone his ceremony so he could remain with his wife. Three days later she died.

"Because of the timing of her illness we couldn't do it then. The night they raised the banner— it was a Saturday night—the Leafs were playing the Montreal Canadiens. My kids Ryan, Meaghan, and Ashley were with me. It was very emotional.

"I asked the Leafs if we could put her signature on the bottom of the banner. It was very important to me. Wendy was obviously a big part of my career. She was the most influential person in my life. And on the charity side, she was recognized by the fans and media as being a big part of it.

"Ryan's draft day, the Hall of Fame, the 10-point night, they're all nice. But when I look back, that moment, that night—it was televised coast to coast on *Hockey Night in Canada*—was special. It kind of brought all of it together.

"Growing up, the Canadiens were my favourite team. Jean Beliveau was my idol. The weekend Wendy died the Leafs were in Montreal. I can remember making the call to [then Leafs' executive] Bill Watters to tell them the news. Then the night the banner goes up, it's Montreal again. It's ironic how those things fall. But I guess if your eyes and ears and heart are open, there might be a reason for things happening.

"The night it went up Tiger [Williams] and Lanny [McDonald] were there, too. They were linemates, but they were and still are close friends. And Lanny's wife, Ardelle, was there and she was very close to Wendy. So that made it special, too. I don't know, but when I reflect on my career there were a lot of good memories, but that night is the most special. They were honouring me, but we honoured Wendy as well. She was there in spirit."

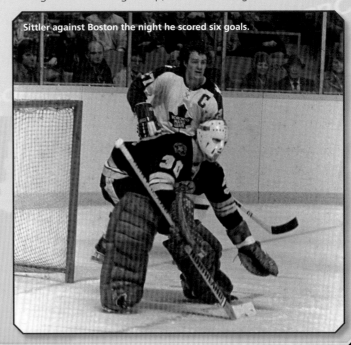

Sittler against Boston the night he scored six goals.

In his first NHL game—in the arena he grew up in, watching the Boston Bruins—Paul Stewart had a hat trick. Ah, well, not your normal hat trick. That night, called up by the Quebec Nordiques from the minors, in his hometown, Stewart fought three legendary heavyweights from the Bruins—Terry O'Reilly, Stan Jonathon, and Al Secord. All in the first period.

"That was my greatest day. I grew up in Boston and like any young boy who grew up in Toronto or Montreal or Ottawa, you want to make it to the NHL from the time you put skates on. My entire goal was to become a player in the NHL. Of course, there weren't many American players prior to the Olympic Miracle On Ice in 1980."

A tough-as-nails competitor, Stewart started as a pro with Binghamton of the North American Hockey League in 1975. He spent time in the minors before landing with Edmonton and Cincinnati in the World Hockey Association. When the WHA merged with the NHL in 1979, the Quebec Nordiques picked up Stewart in the Dispersal Draft. He played 21 games with the Nordiques that season, but it's his first that he'll never forget.

"Fulfilling my dream to play in the NHL, in that building. It was quite a night. [Wayne] Cashman and I got into it with the sticks in the warm up. After I was skating by he stuck me and I chased him down into his end. We had a pre-game moment. For American Thanksgiving Day, we set the table, so to speak."

Stewart's role that night was crystal clear. He was called up as protection playing against the big, bad Bruins. "[Robbie] Ftorek, who was my teammate in Cincinnati in the WHA, two nights prior, well, [Bruin] Bobby Schmautz ran at Ftorek and he got his stick up and cut Schmautz for 20 or 30 stitches and several teeth.

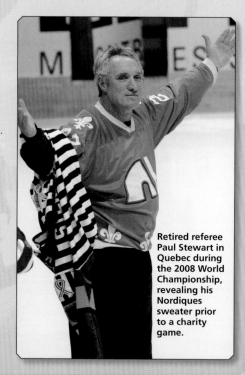

Retired referee Paul Stewart in Quebec during the 2008 World Championship, revealing his Nordiques sweater prior to a charity game.

"And the Bruins being the way that they were had promised that they were going to take it out on Ftorek in the next game. [Nordiques' coach Jacques] Demers and [general manager] Maurice Filion had sent me to Cincy when they got me in the Dispersal Draft. They already had [Curt] Brackenbury and [Wally] Weir doing the job in Quebec City, adding the muscle. I'm not sure they were doing the job as well, or perhaps they knew they were going into Boston and they had their hands full.

"But they called me up. Not only was I getting a chance to play in the National Hockey League in my first game, but also in an arena I grew up watching the

As a referee, Paul Stewart had another greatest day in hockey. It happened on Friday, November 13, 1998, when he refereed a game between the Pittsburgh Penguins and the New Jersey Devils. It was his first game back in the NHL after being diagnosed with colon cancer. "It was a homecoming that, when I was diagnosed with stage 3½ colon cancer on February 23, 1998, was somewhat in doubt. Jaromir Jagr hugged me at centre ice before the game started. [NHL commissioner] Gary Bettman, [NHL public relations man] Frank Brown, and [Devils' GM] Lou Lamoriello made it very special for my family and me. As a person, after that, in September 2001, I had been told that I had both pancreatic cancer and cancer of the throat and that I was going to die. After a PET scan and a throat exam, it turned out that I was not sick again. I ran from the doctor's office and practically flew down the steps of the

Referee Paul Stewart.

hospital. Immediately, I took my son McCauley John Stewart, who was three years old, to the old Boston Arena, where my grandfather had reffed in the NHL back in the 1920s, where my dad had skated his first strides when he was a boy, and where I took my first strides in November 1958, with my sister's too big, white figure skates with a toe pick. Coach Crowder of Northeastern University gave us the ice and McCauley took his first strides on his skates which weren't white, that fit comfortably, and had no toe pick. We then went for a cheese pizza at the Pleasant Cafe. If I had gotten bad news, I wanted to have this memory for McCauley and me. These are three big days in my life that are worth mentioning when I look back. Hockey and skating have been a constant in my life. I am a very lucky guy." Fittingly, the Boston native officiated his last NHL game on April 5, 2003, in his hometown.

Debut Dance with Three

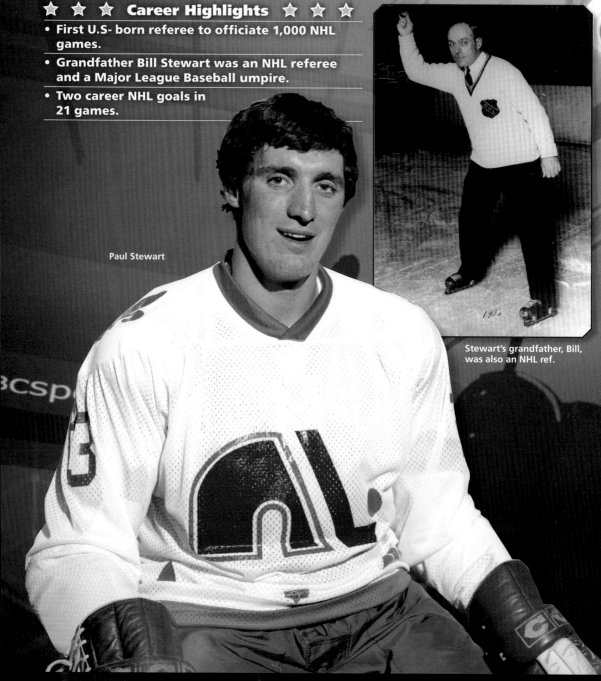

- First U.S- born referee to officiate 1,000 NHL games.
- Grandfather Bill Stewart was an NHL referee and a Major League Baseball umpire.
- Two career NHL goals in 21 games.

Paul Stewart

Stewart's grandfather, Bill, was also an NHL ref.

Bruins. It was a fairytale come true and certainly for me the culmination of all the work and all the things I had to do to get there, which included all the bus rides.

"We got to Boston on the 22nd and I skated with Northeastern University in the morning. Fern Flaman was the coach and I told all the boys to tune in because it was going to be a heckuva night. I walked into the [Garden] and [Bruin] Bobby Miller, who I had played high school hockey against and had known for a long time, was walking up the runway the same time as I was. He was sort of surprised to see me and he says, 'What are you doing here?' I said, 'I want you to go into the dressing room and get all those guys out, [John] Wensink, O'Reilly, Jonathon, Secord and tell them if they want a piece of Ftorek tonight they're going to have to go through me and we might as well start it now, or we can do it whenever.'

"Back in those days, in 1979, they were the big, bad Bruins and Quebec was new trying to get into it a little bit. And I had to do what I had to do. I had done it all those years prior in the WHA and the North American League and the American Hockey League, and I didn't shy away from doing my job. Cashman in the warm up, the "hat trick" in the first period. They certainly knew who I was when I left the Garden. Merci coach Demers, Maurice Filion, owner Marcel Aubut, Robbie Ftorek, and Bobby Schmautz, who took one in the mouth on November 20th and helped make it all possible."

Stewart's NHL playing career lasted just 20 more games, all that season with Quebec. "It says 21 games in the NHL, but that was in the Alan Eagleson NHL. I dressed for 60 games and never touched the ice and when you don't touch the ice you don't get a game credit. That's the way it was in those days."

Stewart finished with two goals and 74 penalty minutes.

"My first goal was the winning goal in Vancouver. Marc Tardif, our great centre, tapped the puck out to me and I made a move on the goaltender, Gary Bromley. He went to the left, but the puck stayed going to the right and you could read NHL on it as it was going across the line. Every kid wants a high hard one, up where the peanut butter is, but mine just trickled across the line. My other one was against the New York Islanders and Chico Resch, who let's just say, had a full head of hair until I scored on him."

The Boston Garden also turned out to be the site of Stewart's first game as an NHL referee, when he subbed for an injured Dave Newell in a Montreal-Boston game on March, 27, 1986. He also worked the final game at the Garden in 1995. His 1,000th game also took place in Boston the night Stewart became the first American-born referee to hit that milestone.

Not surprisingly, given his background, he also appeared in the famous movie *Slapshot*. "I played in Binghamton of the North American Hockey League, which was the forerunner for *Slapshot*. I had 42 fights in 44 games in that 1975–76 season. I'm not sure what happened in those two games I didn't get into a fight— I must have had the night off.

"But they shot the film in Johnstown, Pennsylvania. They were out casting for the different extras and at the time I had a black eye, about 20 stitches, and was missing a few teeth. Art Newman, Paul's brother, was taking pictures to see who they were going to pick and he just looked at me and said, 'You're perfect.'"

P.J. Stock

Student Gets Big Chance

All Philip Joseph Stock wanted was to get an education. In a bizarre twist, his dedication to school got him to the National Hockey League. After playing two years of junior with his hometown Victoriaville Tigres, Stock was not drafted by an NHL team, so he decided to attend St. Francis Xavier University in Antigonish, Nova Scotia, and play university hockey.

"I never thought I would play pro hockey at the time. But it was all because of [former New York Rangers' coach] Colin Campbell. He convinced me to come play and sign as a free agent. He said I might have a chance to play pro hockey. The Rangers put in my contract that they would pay for my education if after two years I left. And I didn't get my signing bonus, which was $22,500, till the second year, so it was all to try to keep me around.

"I thought, I'll play two years. I'm 22 years old. I'll make $75,000 U.S.—remember, it was 60 cents on the dollar then—I'll come back home and continue with my education that's paid for. That was my thought process. I did it, never expecting to play a game in the AHL, let alone the NHL. Then, 17 games into playing with an AHL team [Hartford] that I was surprised I made, I got called up to the Rangers. I think Ryan VandenBussche got hurt. What a day. It was my greatest day.

"They flew me to Carolina. You get off the plane and there is a guy holding a sign with my name on it, a limo driver. He brings me to the rink and you meet everyone. You know, you see all these people on TV, you play with them at training camp, but you never think you'll be in the same room with them. It's game day, game time, and I walk in. You look around the room, the faces— you're so nervous, you don't know what to say. You meet them in training camp, but a lot of that is just going through the motions, handshakes and hellos, but now you're one of 20 guys who are inside that dressing room.

"Wayne Gretzky, Adam Graves, Mike Richter, Brian Leetch, Jeff Beukeboom, the entire group of guys you grew up watching—a bunch of those '80s Oilers guys— Richter, Leetch, the names that were hockey. Superstars.

"Now you're in the same room with them. I didn't know how to prepare for pro hockey. You sit down. You see Gretzky in his pajamas having a coffee. It was awesome. I was so excited to play the game, but I think I was more excited just to hang out with the guys and see what they did. Gretzky has his sticks all lined up a certain way. There are the elite guys who do things separate than the rest."

And then it was game time, and number 28 for the Rangers is a guy who was playing college hockey in a seaside town with a population of 6,000. Even in Carolina at the time there were more people than that in the stands.

"I took a penalty, but not on my first shift. I was just too excited. I went to hit a guy and left my feet. I remember, David Karpa came over to hit me and I faked a dive and Karpa took a minor penalty, too. I have a tape of the game. John Davidson and Sam Rosen are the announcers, and they're talking about how smart of a player I was to do it. That night I played centre with Darren Langdon and Bill Berg. I probably played four or five minutes. It was hands down the best day.

Stock (left) with Boston.

His hands were used more for fighting than scoring. Indeed, he scored only five goals in his NHL career, so they aren't hard to remember, especially the first. It came on February 2, 1998, against the Sharks in San Jose. Stock, who joked about always dreaming of the highlight-reel goal, pushed in a loose puck in the third period to give the New York Rangers a 3–0 lead over the Sharks. In fact, San Jose scored twice before the night was over, making Stock's goal the game winner. After starting the year in the minors, he had played 21 games for the Rangers with one assist before scoring his goal. And the goaltender that night? None other than Kelly Hrudey.

⭐ ⭐ ⭐ **Career Highlights** ⭐ ⭐ ⭐

- One website credits him with 55 regular-season fights in the NHL.
- Finished with 523 penalty minutes in 235 NHL games.
- Accrued 432 penalty minutes in 67 games in his final season of junior in Victoriaville.

P.J. Stock fighting for the puck as a member of the Canadiens.

"And after the game your stuff gets taken away. They take your bag. In the minors you pack your own bag and carry it to the bus. Here we are on the plane, leather seats, and the first thing I had was a shrimp cocktail. I had never flown until I played pro hockey. I flew to St. Francis, but that was the first time I had flown as a player and now I'm on a private jet, playing cards with Gretzky. It's hard to put into words."

Stock, though small, was a hard-nosed, scrappy player, not afraid to fight. He wound up staying a couple of weeks with the Rangers and was called up several more times that season, playing 38 games in all.

After three seasons going up and down from Hartford to the Rangers, he signed as a free agent with the Montreal Canadiens in July 2000, but was traded shortly after with a sixth-round draft pick to Philadelphia for Gino Odjick. At the end of that season, he re-signed with the Rangers as a free agent but was claimed by Boston in the Waiver Draft, playing parts of three seasons with the Bruins before retiring in 2004.

Stock finished with five goals, 26 points, and 523 penalty minutes, appearing in 235 more NHL games than he ever dreamed was possible when he'd enrolled in university eight years earlier.

Stock with the AHL's Hartford Wolf Pack.

Jose Theodore

A Rare Hart and Vezina Double

Funny, but for a lot of players the first game in the NHL is often the greatest day because even if there isn't a second game, it still means you made it. Jose Theodore looks at it a little differently.

"I could say that my greatest day in hockey was my very first game played in the NHL, but just because you play one game doesn't mean you are going to stick around that long."

So one game does not make a greatest day, at least in his eyes, but one season certainly can lead to one.

Selected 44th overall by the Montreal Canadiens in 1994, the Laval native had a terrific junior career leading Hull to the Memorial Cup and earning top-goaltender honours with Team Canada while winning gold at the 1996 World Junior Championship.

After spending parts of three seasons shuttling back and forth between the farm team in Fredericton and the NHL team in Montreal, he finally gained full-time employment with the Canadiens in 1999. He appeared in 30 games and had five shutouts.

The following season, an injury to Jeff Hackett forced the Canadiens to play Theodore more than they had planned. He appeared in 59 games, winning 20. He also became just the second goaltender in NHL history to earn a shutout and score a goal in the same game. That happened January 2, 2001, against the New York Islanders.

But in 2001–02, Theodore became a star. He started 67 games, winning 30, recorded seven shutouts, and had a crisp 2.11 goals-against average. His .931 save percentage was tops in the NHL, and he led Montreal to the playoffs after a three-year absence. All of which culminated in his greatest day.

"My greatest day in hockey was the 2002 NHL Awards show when I won both the Vezina and the Hart Trophies. Playing in the NHL was a dream come true for me. Of course, it is every kid's dream to also win the Stanley Cup. Although the dream of winning the Stanley Cup hasn't happened for me yet, I would have to say my greatest day in hockey would be the night I won both the Vezina and the Hart Trophy."

It was quite a night. The voting for both awards was the closest ever, with each vote ending in a tie and the league having to institute a tie-breaking procedure that hadn't been used in the 48 years it had been in the books.

In the voting for the Hart, which was done by members of the Professional Hockey Writers' Association, Theodore finished tied with Calgary star Jarome Iginla, each with 434 points. Theodore won because he had three more first-place votes. Interestingly, earlier that same day, Iginla won the Lester B. Pearson award, which goes to the most valuable player as voted by the players.

In the Hart voting, Colorado goaltender Patrick Roy, who deemed that season his best, finished third. Theodore's win marked just the sixth time a goaltender had won the award.

Meantime, in the voting for the Vezina, which was done by NHL general managers, both Theodore and Roy finished with 105 points, but Theodore won again because he had 15 first-place votes, three more than Roy.

"It was a great night in Toronto, where I was able to celebrate with my family and my girlfriend Stephanie. Patrick Roy is one of my heroes and he had such a strong season that year for Colorado.

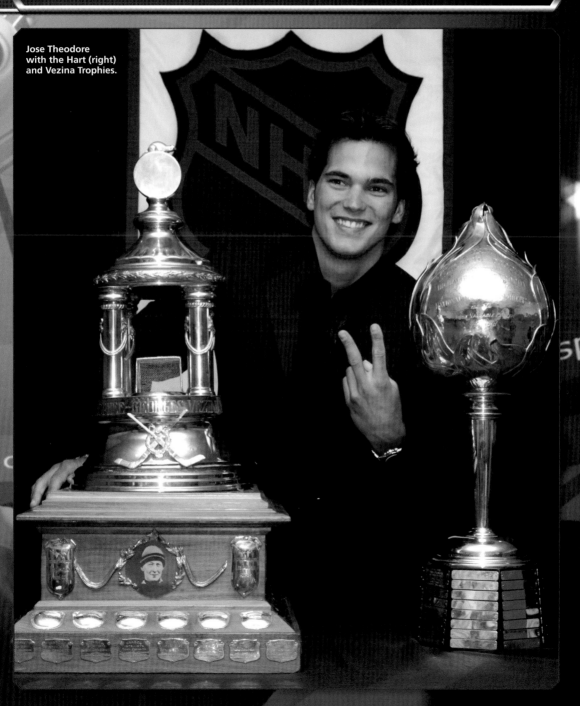

Jose Theodore
with the Hart (right)
and Vezina Trophies.

A Rare Hart and Vezina Double

⭐ ⭐ ⭐ **Career Highlights** ⭐ ⭐ ⭐

• Won the Vezina and Hart Trophies in 2002.
• Scored a goal against the New York Islanders on January 2, 2001.
• Member of Canada's gold-medal winning world junior team in 1996 and was the championship's top goaltender.

Theodore with the Colorado Avalanche.

There are a great many great hockey players whose careers read like storybooks. Jose Theodore is not one of them. Theodore had a brush with scandal when he tested positive after a drug test prior to the 2002 Olympic Games. It was a false alarm as he actually tested for a hair-growth product for which he had a legal prescription and had been taking for more than eight years. He had a much celebrated breakup with his fiancée allegedly because he was seen with celebrity Paris Hilton. He had to watch as his father and his step-brother pleaded guilty to loan sharking and weapon possession while police and some in the media tried to link him to his family's actions. But through all of that, Theodore never stopped trying to excel as a goalie. He is one of only a handful of goalies who have ever shot the puck into an opponent's net, and he did it while posting a shutout versus the New York Islanders. He's won a Vezina and a Hart Trophy in the same season and he had a standout international career having played in the World Juniors, the World Championships, and the World Cup of Hockey.

To beat him out for the league's best goalie still doesn't seem completely right to me. When I won the Vezina, I thought that was unbelievable and it didn't matter what happened after that."

But then Wayne Gretzky, doing the presenting, announced that Theodore had won the Hart.

"I was shaking. I was so excited. Jarome Iginla was a machine that year for Calgary and he was the odds-on favourite for the Hart Trophy. Both were very tight races and I certainly didn't think that I had a chance of winning. I thought the Vezina was Patrick's and that Iggy had the Hart in his pocket. I was just happy to get invited. When my name was read out for both trophies, I was nervous, excited, and stunned. It was a long, tiring year in Montreal, with lots of pressure, but in the end it was worth it to win those two trophies."

Sadly for Theodore, there haven't been many great days since that night. He struggled the next season, although he did bounce back the following year. But after the lockout Theodore had trouble finding his game again and, with the pressure and the frustrations mounting in Montreal, was traded to Colorado—just like his hero Roy a few years before him—in March 2006.

Unlike Roy, however, being in the rarified air of Colorado didn't revive his game entirely. And there was no Stanley Cup. After two inconsistent seasons, Theodore signed with Washington as a free agent in July 2008, although that last season in Colorado was better, as he showed signs of his old form, starting 20 of the final 21 games after starting the year as a back up.

Theodore makes a save.

The First Leaf to 50

The thing that amazed Rick Vaive the most about his greatest day in hockey was that no other Maple Leaf player had experienced it before him, at least while playing in Toronto.

"You think of all the great players who played before me and wore that Maple Leaf—I was surprised no one had done it before."

Strange, but true. Until March 24, 1982, no other Toronto Maple Leaf had scored 50 goals in a season. Then Vaive did it that night against the St. Louis Blues in a 4–3 win at Maple Leaf Gardens.

"That was my greatest day in hockey, scoring my 50th goal. I'll never forget that day and becoming the first Leaf ever to do it. Looking back on it, with all the great players, I kept wondering why I ever had that opportunity to do it. But it's something I'm very proud of and when you're the first person to accomplish something, it's always very special."

The goal arrived in the first period and the picture of the moment was captured on the Leafs' media guide the next season. "I remember the goal like it was yesterday. Billy Derlago, my centre, did all the work. He stickhandled from the blue line all the way into the St. Louis zone. We were on a power play. I kind of hung around on my off side, the left side, and he threaded a perfect backhand pass across the top of the crease. All I had to do was one-time it.

"Okay, I had to pick the top corner, but Billy did all the work. Mike Liut was the goalie and I never let him forget. He tried to get over, but I managed to get it up. I have a beautiful picture of it and the defenceman going down to try to block the shot was Guy Lapointe, so that was special, that a great player like Guy Lapointe would be in the picture. I have a lot of great memories in my career, my life, even before I got to pro hockey, but that was the most special. I still have the puck, at home, in my office."

Vaive with the Leafs.

It was in the 75th game in an 80-game season that Vaive scored number 50. But it was in the 74th game that he accelerated the hunt and actually set the Leaf record, surpassing Frank Mahovlich's 48 goals scored in 1961.

"The game before I scored four goals against Chicago at Maple Leaf Gardens. What was kind of funny is the last two were from around the blueline on Tony Esposito. I was shooting from there because I knew he couldn't see any of the long ones any more. His eyes were bad, so if you didn't hit him, it was going in because he couldn't react until he saw it at the last second.

"It was nice that night to get the four because it took some of the pressure off. There were still six games left to get the

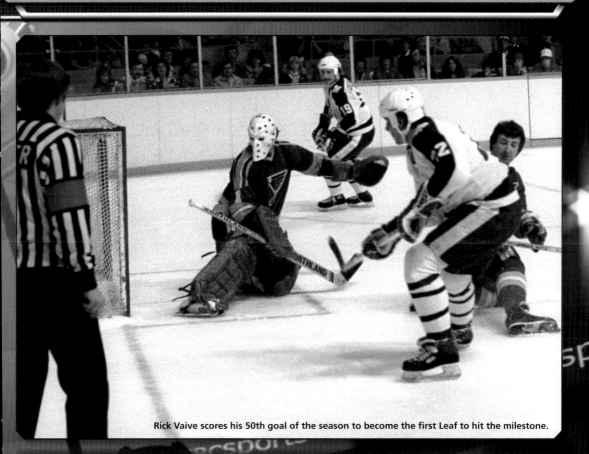

Rick Vaive scores his 50th goal of the season to become the first Leaf to hit the milestone.

Back in the 1978–79 season, Rick Vaive became a Bull—a Baby Bull to be precise. After a 78-goal season with Sherbrooke in junior, Vaive signed with the Birmingham Bulls of the World Hockey Association as a 19-year-old. The Bulls' owner, John Bassett, was in desperate need of talent and decided to sign junior players who hadn't reached the NHL draft age of 20. Vaive was one of seven teenagers he signed for $50,000 each. Six, including Vaive, made the team. The others were defencemen Craig Hartsburg, Rob Ramage, and Gaston Gingras, along with forward Michel Goulet and goaltender Pat Riggin. That summer, after the NHL and WHA merged, all were selected in the NHL Entry Draft, the first in which the age of eligibility was reduced. That year it was 19, the following year 18.

★ ★ ★
Career Highlights
★ ★ ★

- In 13 NHL seasons, he had 441 goals and 788 points.

- Played in three NHL All-Star Games.

- Twice played for Canada at the World Championships.

Leafs' captain Rick Vaive.

50th. And those four goals got me to 49, so I was able to pass Frank. So it was like I had two special nights."

Typically, at the time, the Leafs were not enjoying a good season and the owner, the late Harold Ballard, was in a prickly mood. As such, apart from the celebration that night on the ice, the Leafs didn't do anything to honor Vaive at the time.

"I enjoyed the moment as much as I could. On the personal side, I enjoyed it with family, but unfortunately it wasn't a great time in Leaf history. I do remember Harold Ballard not doing anything. Not doing a night, nothing. I think at the time he was upset because he had done things to honour guys like Darryl Sittler and he had moved on, so he wasn't going to do that any more. Who knows?

"The person who was the most upset was my wife, Joyce. I really didn't think about it, I was just so happy to score 50 goals in the National Hockey League and be the first Leaf ever to do it. But she was really ticked off. She went to a jeweler friend of ours and designed a beautiful Maple Leaf ring that no one else has. She was teaching at the time, paid for it herself, and she gave it to me and said it was to remember that goal. That was pretty special."

As it turned out, there was an owner who honoured Vaive that year. It was the owner of a restaurant near the Gardens, which the players used to frequent after practice.

"It was called Mr. Greenjeans. And they used to have these 36-ounce drafts. Well, one day the owner came over to our table and said, 'if you score 50, I'll give you 50 drafts. The big ones.' When the season was over, my best buddies, Billy Derlago, John Anderson, Greg Terrion, and our wives went there for dinner and, well, we finished them off."

Vaive, who was 22 years old that season, finished with 54 goals, a club record that still stands. He went on to score 51 goals the next season and 52 the year after that.

"All of that was great, personally, but the goal was to win the Stanley Cup as a Leaf, and we didn't do that. There were some tough seasons."

After a high-scoring junior career with the Sherbrooke Beavers, Vaive joined the Birmingham Bulls of the World Hockey Association as a 19-year-old. He spent one year as a "Baby Bull," as the under-age kids were called, then was drafted fifth overall by the Vancouver Canucks. Midway through his first season in Vancouver, in 1979–80, Vaive and Derlago were traded to the Leafs in exchange for Dave "Tiger" Williams and Jerry Butler.

Vaive and Derlago, quite often with Anderson on the left wing, enjoyed considerable success playing together through some tough years for a team beset by the meddling of Ballard. Vaive was named Leafs' captain at age 22, then had the "C" taken away in 1986 after he slept through an early morning practice on the road. He was traded to Chicago, along with Steve Thomas and Bob McGill in 1987, in exchange for Al Secord and Ed Olczyk.

He played well for the Blackhawks for a few seasons before being traded to Buffalo and finishing his NHL career there in 1992. Vaive, who was a power right winger with a big slap shot, wasn't afraid to fight. He finished his career with 441 goals, but it is the 50 he scored in 1981–82 that led to his greatest day in hockey.

Olympic Gold Forever

When you've been called the female Wayne Gretzky, when you've won World Championship and Olympic gold medals, and when you were the first woman to play professional hockey full time, well, there is no shortage of great moments.

And so it is with Hayley Wickenheiser, who has twice won Olympic gold, once won Olympic silver, and six times brought home World Championship golds. She also twice attended rookie camps for the Philadelphia Flyers and played parts of a couple of seasons with a pro team in Finland. On top of all that, she is the first female to participate in team sports in both the Winter and Summer Olympics, in hockey and softball.

That's just scratching the surface of Wickenheiser's sporting resume, but you get the idea. Ultimately, though, her greatest day was one many didn't expect to materialize.

"The greatest day was winning the gold medal in 2002 in Salt Lake City and doing it with the team that we had. We had lost every single game to the Americans leading up to the Olympics. We were 0-and-8 going into that final game. And to beat them on their home soil...

"The emotion surrounding what was going on with the men's team, we felt like we were in it together and to win it and see the men do it a few days later was emotional and probably the greatest day that I have ever experienced."

The men's team had its struggles in the tournament but battled through to the final, beating the Americans, 5–2. And the women had lost all eight exhibition games dating back to August, 2001. Then, in that gold-medal game, things changed, although the challenge and the adversity remained the same.

Canada took a 1–0 lead less than two minutes into the game. After the Americans tied it early in the second, Wickenheiser scored at 4:10 to give Canada a lead it wouldn't surrender. They expanded that lead to 3–1 heading into the final period. Although the Americans scored again late in the game, Canada managed to hang on, but not without enduring an endless run of penalties that included a couple of 5-on-3 advantages for the Americans.

On the night, the Canadians were shorthanded 11 times—including eight straight—and the Americans just four times. All the Americans could muster were two power-play goals, and they failed to score the equalizer with an advantage with 3:56 left in the third period.

"I remember turning to Vicky Sunohara and Dana Antal on the bench in the third period. We had a name our team was going to use if we ran into poor refereeing. The name was 'Emerald Lake.' It was a lodge we had gone to in B.C. as a retreat before we went to the Olympics, and we talked about all the distractions that could possibly happen. One of those distractions was bad refereeing in the final game. And I remember turning to them and saying that, 'Emerald Lake,' and we started laughing. It was in the middle of the third period and it took the tension away. They [the Americans] started to get tense. They weren't scoring on the power play, and we started to relax on

Of the many accomplishments in her career, Hayley Wickenheiser has one that is truly unique. She was the first woman to record a point in a men's professional hockey game, in 2003, assisting on a goal while playing for Salamat in the Finnish League. Almost 13 minutes into the game, Wickenheiser won a faceoff. The puck went back to the point where defenceman Matti Tevanen shot and scored in a 7–3 win. Wickenheiser didn't score and had a quiet game overall, although she did accidentally put the puck in her own net late in the game. Wickenheiser was the second woman skater to play in a men's pro game. In 1998–99, Maren Valenti played 24 games for Freiburg of Germany's second division. In the summer of 2008, Wickenheiser signed a one-year contract with Eskilsuna, a third-division men's team in Sweden.

Wickenheiser with Olympic gold.

Olympic Gold Forever

★ ★ ★ **Career Highlights** ★ ★ ★

- **Won an Olympic gold medal in Salt Lake City in 2002 and Turin in 2006.**
- **Won an Olympic silver medal in Nagano in 1998.**
- **Six-time world champion (1994, 1997, 1999, 2000, 2001, and 2004).**

Wickenheiser fights off two American players.

the penalty kill. We almost embraced every penalty we got as an advantage for us. It kind of changed the mentality and it was a way for us to get through that game."

And so they did, hanging on to win, 3–2, the first Olympic gold for either the men or women since 1952. Three days later, of course, the men would end a 50-year wait with a 5–2 win over the Americans. Wickenheiser, who shared the tournament scoring lead, was named most valuable player.

"When it was over, I just remember being relieved. I remember being so excited, but also relieved. You're happy your family is there. You're close to home, so everybody can share it with you. The excitement of representing Canada and the emotion of all that. I remember that literally a few seconds later thinking, 'Oh my God, we've got to do this again in four years.' You go through that whole range of emotions. It lasts for maybe just a few moments and then you almost move on. It was certainly every emotion that day.

Hayley bites her gold medal.

"I remember watching those seconds tick down—five, four, three—and being so happy that we won, but also thinking, I'm really happy this is over, too. In a way, because of all the turmoil or adversity that our team had faced throughout the year and being able to pull it out and win in really an underdog situation, where we had been written off as a team, was incredible. I've been in both situations where you're expected to win and when you're not. That one was certainly the most emotional. When you win, you don't want it to end.

"In the dressing room, there were so many people who came in. Pat Quinn, Kevin Lowe, and Wayne Gretzky were there. I came into the room, opened the door, and Wayne and Kevin were standing there and I was first back in the dressing room. I walked right past them I was so happy and excited, then I turned and realized they were there and Wayne said, 'Well, that was a close one. I knew you guys were going to win all the way.'

"Pat Quinn was very emotional. He was pretty much in tears on the bench. It kind of hit him how our coaching staff had so much composure throughout the game. I remember him saying he would have lost it long ago. I think it kind of inspired the men a little unexpectedly. They took that emotion from that win.

"After that, I remember just sitting there and talking with all the girls, people who had shared the journey. Then you go meet your family and friends. I certainly enjoyed that for a few days. And then you go back to Calgary, where we had centralized as a team, and now all the girls have to spread out and go across Canada and there is an emptiness there. It's like an Olympic hangover, an Olympic depression you go into after you go through something like that, but you never forget how good winning it was."

Photo Credits

Hockey Hall of Fame/Robert Shaver—p. 14, 38, 43, 82, 123 (left), 150, 168, 191, 193, 206, 208

Hockey Hall of Fame/Dave Sandford—p. 16, 37, 44 (bottom), 48 (top), 68 (left, bottom right), 75, 93, 94, 98, 121, 124, 140, 146, 163, 164, 182

Hockey Hall of Fame—IIHF/Dave Sandford—p. 35, 36 (bottom), 62, 65, 148, 211, 212, 213

Hockey Hall of Fame/Doug MacLellan—p. 17, 59, 87, 92, 108, 117, 136 (inset), 144 (right), 153

Hockey Hall of Fame/Graphic Artists—p. 24, 58, 76 (both), 110, 112 (both), 155, 156 (right), 196 (bottom)

Hockey Hall of Fame/Lewis Portnoy—p. 25, 31 (left), 32 (inset), 51, 60 (both), 84, 167, 183

Hockey Hall of Fame Archives—p. 28, 30, 44 (top), 104 (left), 138, 196 (inset)

Hockey Hall of Fame/Paul Bereswill—p. 29, 39, 50, 52, 53, 64, 68 (top right), 86, 88, 91, 104 (right), 114, 116 (both), 122, 123 (inset), 131, 134, 135, 136 (left), 139 (right), 144 (inset), 152, 171, 174, 175, 176, 180, 184, 187, 188

Hockey Hall of Fame/Turofsky Collection—p. 31 (right), 32 (left), 83, 99, 100

Hockey Hall of Fame/Paul Bettings—p. 34

Hockey Hall of Fame/Walt Neubrand—p. 46, 47, 139 (inset), 166

Hockey Hall of Fame/Steve Deschênes—p. 54

Hockey Hall of Fame/Phil Pritchard—p. 70, 120, 178

Hockey Hall of Fame/Craig Campbell—p. 78, 79, 80 (both), 81

Hockey Hall of Fame/Frank Prazak—p. 111, 156 (inset), 192

Hockey Hall of Fame/Matthew Manor—p. 127

Hockey Hall of Fame—IIHF/Matthew Manor—p. 147, 158, 194, 195

Hockey Hall of Fame—IIHF/Jukka Rautio—p. 160

Hockey Hall of Fame/Bill Wellman—p. 128

Hockey Hall of Fame/Chris Relke—p. 141

Hockey Hall of Fame/Fred Keenan—p. 154

Hockey Hall of Fame/Lorne Sandler—p. 157

Hockey Hall of Fame/Mike Bolt—p. 162, 179

Hockey Hall of Fame/Steve Babineau—p. 201

Reuters—15, 19, 20 (left), 20 (right), 23, 27, 36 (inset), 40, 48 (bottom), 55, 56, 63, 67, 71, 72, 85, 95, 96, 107, 119, 129, 159, 161, 165, 169, 185, 190, 199, 200, 203, 204, 205

Graig Abel—p. 105, 115, 151, 207

Getty Images—p. 65, 132, 143, 170, 172

Hockey Night in Canada—p. 189

Hockey Canada—p. 103

Scott Morrison is a 27-year veteran hockey journalist and recipient of the Hockey Hall of Fame's 2006 Elmer Ferguson Memorial Award. Scott appears on the Satellite Hot Stove each week on CBC's *Hockey Night in Canada,* as well as contributing pre-game and intermission features and writing regularly for cbcsports.ca. A highly respected hockey journalist, the Toronto native began his career at the *Toronto Sun* in 1979. After spending more than 11 years as a hockey writer and columnist at the paper, Morrison became Sports Editor in 1991 and led the section to being named one of North America's top-10 sports sections in 1999—the first sports section in Canada to receive the AP Sports Editors North American Award. Morrison has authored several hockey books and served two terms as President of the Professional Hockey Writers' Association.

CBC's *Hockey Night in Canada* has been a national institution since 1952, when Foster Hewitt's familiar "Hello, Canada!" ushered hockey fans into the era of television. Now in its 54th season on television, it remains the most popular weekly sports program in Canada, averaging more than one million viewers every Saturday night.